Praise for
THE HEROINES CLUB

The world is overwhelmed with resources on connecting to our babies and younger children. Information on "how to manage" older children abounds. The Heroines Club is unique. It offers a simple and powerful way to stay in positive, deep, lifelong connection to our daughters. The simple and transparent methods in this book embody principles of compassionate communication that build trust and empathy in our most intimate relationships, rather than "managing people." While recognizing, honoring and supporting the role of women in creating healthy societies, The Heroines Club also helps us create communication and relationship that respect the dignity of others at any age. I believe all mothers want mutually nurturing relationships with our daughters. This book shows us how to be intentional about sustaining the strong yet sometimes fragile connections among women, rather than leaving things to chance. The Heroines Club resonated with me on a deep intellectual, emotional and spiritual level.

Janet Jendron, President of Attachment Parenting International

Melia Keeton-Digby has created a wise ritual, rooted in ancient practices and invoking the issues of our times. The Heroines Club brings relational sensitivity and a fierce fighting spirit to the support of mother–daughter bonding, the creation of community, the calling forth of the Motherline and the honoring of a pantheon of heroines who inspire women's empowerment as well as their psychological, and spiritual development. A blessing for women and girls, I hope The Heroines Club will travel the world.

Naomi Ruth Lowinsky Ph.D, Jungian analyst,
author of *The Motherline*

In a world that devalues the female from birth, The Heroines Club is a beautiful gift for mothers and daughters to reestablish their worth, power and creativity. I enjoyed reading it myself and look forward to working through the monthly activities with my daughter. A highly recommended read for mothers of girl-children filled with ideas you can easily incorporate into your lives. If you have wanted to begin an empowering mother-daughter circle but were at a loss as to how, The Heroines Club walks you through it seamlessly.

Trista Hendren, author of *The Girl God* series

The Heroines Club represents a joyful and powerful way for mothers and daughters to connect as they draw on the history, knowledge, and wisdom of those who came before us. I would highly recommend it to any mother who is looking for a new and different way to learn and grow with her daughter, either as a dyad or part of a larger group.

Carla Naumburg, PhD, clinical social worker and author of *Parenting in the Present Moment*

The Heroines Club is an indispensable guide for fostering an intimate mother-daughter bond. In my women's health practice, I encounter women struggling with health issues rooted in low self-esteem, inability to advocate for themselves and lack of connection with their bodies. The Heroines Club is real preventative medicine, helping mothers and their daughters to steer clear of these all too common pitfalls through nurturing their inherent intuition.

Keeton-Digby has given her readers the gift of an inspired program that builds on her own deep personal experiences, creating a guide that will foster the mother-daughter dyad to its full healing potential. In this clear and articulate read, she distills her life lessons into an integrated approach that is deceptively simple yet exceedingly rich.

I was moved to share this book with the important women in my life: mother, daughters, sisters and friends. I'm sure you will want to do the same.

Rebecca Lasky Cohen, M.D.

Raising children in our fast-paced, anxiety-fueled culture can lead to paralyzing confusion in parents. Bravo to Melia Keeton-Digby for creating The Heroines Club, an inspired program for mothers and daughters that fosters connection and gives our precious girls license to shine!

Nancy Rose, parenting and life strategist and author of *Raise the Child You've Got—Not the One You Want*

The Heroines Club is truly a must-have book for mothers who wish to foster a deeper connection with their daughters. As mothers, we are our daughters' first teachers, role models, and wise counsel. We have been blessed with a responsibility to nourish spirit and nurture healthy self-esteem, yet many of us were never taught how. This wonderful and easy-to-use guide will inspire and empower mothers to change Herstory through conscious storytelling, ritual, reverence, and the ancient ceremonial practice of the women's circle.

Reading The Heroines Club, I found myself not only nodding, but pausing to clutch it to my heart. This is a book that should be in every woman's hands, and passed down from generation to generation.

Wendy Cook, founder of Mighty Girl Art™

My favorite part of The Heroines Club is the discussion of several amazing women scientists, all of whom have made our world a much better place. Our budding female scientists desperately need more role models! I look forward to discussing these role models with my daughter (and our soon-to-be-launched Heroines Club!) Thank you, Melia, for creating a book that'll enhance my relationship with my daughter, as well as inspire her in the sciences.

Tracy Camp, PhD, Professor of Computer Science

Self-love, self-care, self-acceptance and self-worth! In The Heroines Club, Melia Keeton-Digby guides mothers to remember the art of passing these and other essential gifts to their daughters. These gifts are our birthright and by nature are as powerfully transformative to give as to receive. The process itself is joyful, healing and potent: mothers and daughters are nourished and as well as families and communities. Best of all, this book goes way beyond inspiration by offering a practical, step-by-step guide to preparing and facilitating your Mother-Daughter Empowerment Circle. My daughter loved the Heroines Club too. What a difference our mother-daughter circle made in our lives.

Wherever you are in the world, however your life's journey is unfolding, if mothering a daughter is one of your roles, this book is for you.

**Katharine Krueger, director of
Journey of Young Women: A Coming of Age Community**

The Heroines Club

A Mother-Daughter Empowerment Circle

Melia Keeton-Digby

WOMANCRAFT PUBLISHING

The Heroines Club

© Melia Keeton-Digby 2016

Cover art © Arna Baartz
Typeset and design by Lucent Word, Cork, Ireland

Published by Womancraft Publishing, 2016
www.womancraftpublishing.com

ISBN: 978-1910559-147 (paperback)
ISBN: 978-1910559-154 (Kindle)

The photo of Melia Keeton-Digby with her daughter Della was taken by Amy Bammel Wilding.

A percentage of Womancraft Publishing profits are invested back into the environment reforesting the tropics (via TreeSisters) and forward into the community: providing books for girls in developing countries, and affordable libraries for red tents and women's groups around the world.

Womancraft Publishing is committed to sharing powerful new women's voices, through a collaborative publishing process. We are proud to midwife this work, however, the story, the experiences and the words are the author's alone.

For Della Ruth,
I've loved you since the beginning of time.
Thank you for choosing me.

For River and Brynn,
may you always remember your divinity.

For mothers and daughters everywhere,
we are in this together.

ACKNOWLEDGMENTS

Thank you to the following people—without their contributions and support this book could not have been written.

Rick Digby, my beloved husband and the "Pop" of our children. No matter what I've dreamed up over the years, your first response has always been, "How can I help?" God bless our love.

Lucas, Erick, and Della, my beloved children, who taught me how to love and be loved. Thank you for sharing your mother so generously with the world.

Lindsay Jeffcoat, my first friend, my other half, my sister. I don't know how I accomplished anything in those first four years of life without you.

Amy Bammel Wilding, my best friend and life-partner, who read each chapter along the way, offering much-needed encouragement, insights, and edits. We truly are in this together and for that, I am so thankful. DFTS!

Sean and Rania Woods, for your unwavering love, support, and mad editing skills. Sean, some of our most important conversations have happened while sitting on the driveway, and I'll never forget the one where I told you I wanted to write this book, and you, as always, told me to go for it.

Rosemary and John Digby, for the countless hours of love, care, and car rides you gave your grandchildren while their mama needed to write.

Sandy Woods, my mama, for teaching me to think, write, live, and love with a wide-open heart.

Jim Woods, my dad, for raising me to know I was a "Woods girl."

Glennon Doyle Melton, founder of Momastery and Together Rising and one of my personal heroines, who once wrote, "We can't go around saying it takes a village (to raise a child)—we have to build the damn village!" Your call to action was the spark that ignited the Heroines Club in my soul, and for that I will be forever grateful.

Baraka Elihu, my teacher, who first taught me the art of sacred circling, and who believed in the Heroines Club from the very beginning.

Lucy Pearce of Womancraft Publishing and Lucent Word editing, the skilled midwife that helped me birth this book into being. Working with you has been a dream come true!

The original Heroines Club members: Ashley, Salem, Averlin, Fran, Ella, Linda, Grace, Baraka, Akasha, Cori, Adah, Camille, and Sydney. Thank you for sharing your lives with me and believing in this work.

And finally, to the heroines represented in these pages, and on whose shoulders we stand: thank you. We are because you were.

CONTENTS

No coming, no going,
No after, no before.
I hold you close,
I release you to be free;
I am in you
And you are in me.

Thich Nhat Hạnh

INTRODUCTION

Beloved woman,

If you are hoping to connect with your daughter in meaningful ways;

If you want your daughter to possess the skills and tools she will need for a safe, confident and connected journey into womanhood;

If you believe that it is you, as her mother, alongside a community of other like-minded mothers and daughters, that can best offer her these skills and tools;

If you want your daughter to intimately know the real-life heroines from which she comes;

If you long to build and maintain a relationship with your daughter based on love and mutuality;

Then, dear woman, this book was written for you.

The Heroines Club was created with these desires and goals specifically in mind. Every day our daughters are inundated with images and messages of what a "perfect" girl and woman look like. In our ever-changing and often limiting society, we must show our girls what it truly means to be a woman. We must instill values in them that will resonate as they transition into womanhood. As mothers, we can join arms with one another to offer our daughters an unwavering sense of self-love, hope, and a desire to succeed beyond their imagination.

And may all mothers know that they are loved,

And may all sisters know that they are strong,

And may all daughters know that they are powerful,

That the circle of women may live on.

Mica Ella from "Circle of Women"

The Heroines Club offers a profoundly nourishing and age-appropriate experience for mothers and daughters aged 7+ to share together. Through the study and sharing of women's history with our daughters, we can explore key issues with a razor sharp and potent focus.

The heroines represented in this book and program are athletes, inventors, artists, and revolutionaries, all from different backgrounds, but they have one thing in common—they are strong role models for young girls to learn about, look up to, and be inspired by.

Offering thought-provoking discussion, powerful rituals, and engaging activities, the Heroines Club fortifies our daughters' self-esteem, invigorates our own spirits, and nourishes our relationships. In a culture that can make mothering daughters seem intimidating and isolating, the Heroines Club offers us an antidote.

Through these pages, I will offer you a revolutionary model for empowering your daughter and strengthening your mother-daughter relationship. Whether you are hoping to start a Heroines Club in your community, planning to share it with another close mother/daughter pair, or even hoping to simply do it alone with your daughter, I will lay out a clear, easy-to-use template for building your own Heroines Club to create a safe space in which your daughter can thrive.

The Birth of the Heroines Club

This curriculum is informed by my knowledge and experience as an educator, transformational life coach, and women's circle facilitator. While this curriculum is supported by research and intellectual rigor, it springs directly from the depths of my mother heart.

When my third child and only daughter, Della, was four years old, her experience of life was already very different to that of her brothers'. After raising two sons into adolescence, the stark contrast of how the world interacted with my daughter, almost solely through her physical appearance, was alarming to me. Everywhere we went well-meaning people were viewing my fierce, kind, wise, and creative girl entirely through her physical appearance:

"Good morning! Don't you look pretty today!"

"I love your dress/shirt/shorts/shoes/hair!"

"Hi, princess! Aren't you adorable!"

"You're so cute!"

One indelible morning in particular stood out to me as a proverbial straw. Della and I were participating in a parent/child theater class together and during the drive to class, Della, the avid animal-lover, was perfecting her fiercest lion roar. She was certain that her new teacher would be impressed. As we entered the stage area and greeted our new teacher, Della smiled and gave her best roar. Unfortunately, her teacher missed the opportunity to encourage Della's creative expression, and instead, complimented her on her polka dot tights.

I knew that these people only wanted to engage with Della. They were simply following a distinct script from our culture as to how one does so with a little girl. But each time I would hear Della's compulsory and deflated "thank you," I could almost see the most vital parts of her powerful personhood, the parts I knew she would need most to grow into a whole, empowered, and connected young woman, being utterly cast aside. My daughter was getting the message loud and clear, from multiple directions, that the way she looked was more important than anything else.

Around this time, my oldest son Lucas brought home his eighth grade Social Studies textbook to prepare for a final exam. As I flipped through the pages with him, I was shocked to see an outright lack of women's history being represented. The female half of the world's population has thousands of years of documented history from which to pick, and yet I saw few of our sisters' stories being told! *Where were the women?* Could these losses be tied together somehow? Might this blatant lack of representation be part of the same script I saw acted out with my daughter that morning at theater class and every day in our society?

Professionally, I was also noticing an alarming trend among the female students I served as a speech-language pathologist for our public school system. Over a decade I had watched as confident, out-spoken girls of seven and eight were losing their voices and turning inward in self-consciousness and insecurity by the time they reached eleven or twelve. At what point, I wondered, do our daughters finally just give up and repress their fierce lioness roar so as to fit more easily into the patriarchy's restrictive box labeled "acceptable girlhood"?

Each night I went to bed with one big question in my heart: *how can we intervene before it is too late?*

At the same time as these ruminations, I was deeply invested in my practice of sacred circling, both as a participant and later, as a facilitator. On a particularly gorgeous day in Athens, Georgia, I sat in circle discussing with other women how the process of circling together had changed our lives. I shared that when I was first introduced to this ancient practice years ago, I experienced a joyous home-coming. Buoyed by the love and support of my circle sisters, I learned (or perhaps, *remembered*), what it really means to love myself. I got in touch with the core of my power and was able to spend more time acting from that place. I learned to love and to be loved in a way that only other women can offer. Here was a place where women could come together, bring themselves in their authentic entirety, and be completely held in support and compassion. Belonging to a women's circle had changed my life. My words that day met with nods and affirmations. *Yes, me too.* Tears of gratitude flowed as we recognized that the practice of sacred circling had allowed us to recapture ourselves. Like a life-preserver bobbing in the shifting seas of life, it had offered us something to clutch while we rested and reclaimed the missing parts of ourselves.

In that moment a wave of realization washed over me: circling with our daughters is the ideal prevention model for all that worries us about mothering daughters. Perhaps instead of working to reunite with the lost parts of their powerful personhood, our daughters can maintain that contact from the outset. They can be raised to love themselves, to believe in their inherent worth and power, and to know what it feels like to be supported by a circle of women. My mission became clear . . . and the Heroines Club was born.

From the beginning, the Heroines Club was a success in our community, with circles filling almost immediately. Mothers were grateful for the support and daughters treasured this time together with Mom.

The Heroines Club offers me time to cherish with my daughter. Being part of this experience enriches my ability to be a mother. I get to hear the voices of other mothers, of heroines before me, and decide how I want to mother. By mothering I mean being a strong role model and talking about lessons and character traits I might have otherwise ignored or at least only passively acknowledged. Instead this group gives me the empowerment to mother. The group has prepared me for all the questions that I never expected from my eight-year-old. Being more prepared as a mother has made our relationship more authentic.

I feel that I have gotten to know my daughter and what she is proud of and who she is from the inside. When we check in about what made us proud of ourselves that month, I get to learn about my daughter. Just hearing her makes me know her and thus improves how we communicate. We are learning to give love and receive it because the group has encouraged communication between us.

Linda, Heroines Club Mother

The Heroines Club strengthens me and lets me have a voice. Usually no one listens to me but in the group I get to have a voice. It strengthens me because every time we talk about the heroines I feel like I can do what they did.

Grace, eight years old

The Heroines Club rests on the following convictions

◎ A mother is her daughter's primary and most influential teacher.

◎ With appropriate role models and guidance, daughters can thrive through adolescence and beyond.

◎ Mothers and daughters excel when supported by a community of other mothers and daughters.

◎ The practice of sacred circling acts as a channel to effect true change in ourselves and in our culture.

The Gifts of the Heroines Club

Empowerment: Mothers empower daughters while having their own sense of empowerment recharged.

Mutuality: In sacred circle, the generation gap closes as mothers and daughters join together. Mothers find that there is much they can learn from their daughters and that teaching and learning flow in both directions.

Edification: The Heroines Club helps girls hold on to the parts of themselves that are intuitive, outspoken, and strong, thereby fortifying their girlhood identity, which will serve as the foundation for their future adolescent and adult selves.

Initiation: Daughters learn the art of ritual, reverence, and the powerful, ancient practice of women circling together.

Herstory: By imparting knowledge of *our* past, from a feminist perspective, and emphasizing the role of women as told from a woman's point of view, part of what we accomplish through the Heroines Club is explicitly showing our daughters the full range of who they might become.

Self-Awareness and Confidence: The Heroines Club acts as a preventative model against the most common fears we mothers have for our daughters. A solid sense of self-awareness and self-confidence is one of the greatest tools we can offer our daughters on their journey to womanhood. The heroines chosen for this curriculum offer concrete, real-life examples of these qualities in their highest expressions.

Community: As the African Proverb states, "It takes a village to raise a child." The Heroines Club offers a conscious community of other mothers and daughters to support us in the divine tasks of mothering, daughtering, and growing up.

Bonding: The Heroines Club offers our daughters the vital quality time they crave (and need.) You will share sweet mother-daughter moments that will be cherished by you both.

Conscious Story Telling and Values: By discussing the life of each heroine, honoring them for their strength, passion, perseverance, courage, and self-love, our daughters learn what we value, what we wish for them, and most of all, what is possible for their lives.

I trust you will find a special magic in *The Heroines Club*. Through circling with our daughters in this way, we bless and empower not only our own daughters, but also *their* daughters, and all of the women to come. And the really sweet part? By blessing them, we heal ourselves and all the women who came before us. As psychiatrist and psychotherapist C.G. Jung once said, "Every mother contains her daughter in herself and every daughter her mother, and every mother extends backwards into her mother and forwards into her daughter."

I hope this book serves you well.

In sisterhood,
Melia Keeton-Digby

Part One

The Heroines Club:
Empowering Mothers and
Daughters Together

WHAT IS THE HEROINES CLUB?

It is six o'clock on a warm Friday evening in May. Two by two, mothers and daughters are entering a beautifully prepared space, offering greetings and hugs to one another before taking their seats in circle. There is a collective release, a shared exhale, as mothers set their belongings to the side, slide out of their shoes, and settle into a sacred space with their daughters. The girls are bubbling over with excitement and we hear Averlin (eight years old) say, "Being at the Heroines Club feels like Christmas morning!" We all laugh and agree. Yes! We've made it. We're here together and this is our special time.

In the center of the room, on a low coffee table, sits a framed portrait of this month's honoree heroine, exquisitely illuminated in candlelight. We have spent the past month getting to know this real-life heroine and now as we gaze on her timeless face in the photograph, we feel a deep connection; her energy is present with us in circle tonight. We are invited to close our eyes for the opening meditation and we visualize ourselves, with our loving ancestors behind us, our supportive mothers, daughters, and sisters around us, and our beloved heroine resting in the center. We allow ourselves to pause the events, activities, and responsibilities outside

Imagine a community of women inspiring its daughters to refuse to twist their lives out of shape to fit into expectations; supporting them to refuse to please others by pretending to be less intelligent and gifted than they are; and empowering them to love their woman-bodies, regardless. Imagine yourself as part of this community.

Patricia Lynn Reilly

of this space and time, and land fully present with one another. Breathing together during the short meditation, we become one powerful entity, creating a whole that is greater than the sum of its parts. Welcome to the Heroines Club.

A note card featuring the Heroines Club commitments is tenderly passed around the circle and read aloud:

We are all the teachers and we are all the taught.

We share from our hearts and we speak our truths.

What is said in circle stays in circle.

We respect the space.

We honor our heroines, ourselves, one another, and the mother-daughter relationship.

By speaking these rules, we establish that the space is sacred and our confidentiality is confirmed. We know that we can allow ourselves to be seen and heard in our entirety, trusting that we will be received in support and compassion. We affirm that mothers have as much to learn from their daughters and that in circle, we are equals. We promise to respect the space, knowing that it has been lovingly prepared for our time together. We acknowledge that honoring ourselves is our highest calling, and honoring our heroines is a gift we give ourselves. We venerate the mother-daughter relationship and set the intention to bless our time together.

Our talking stick, crafted from a deer antler and gemstones, is reverently passed around the circle for check-ins. One by one, we listen as each woman and girl shares her response to this month's prompt: "Share something about yourself of which you are especially proud." There is a profound medicine to be had in encouraging our daughters to declare their strengths and gifts, and allowing them to hear us take pride in ours as well. Through this sharing, they hear from us where we place value and we hear from them more of what is happening in their lives. Perhaps even more importantly, our daughters learn that we celebrate our sisters and we are not afraid to shine; there is more than enough for all of us.

Our deepest fear is not that we are inadequate. Our deepest fear is that we are powerful beyond measure. It is our light, not our darkness that most frightens us. We ask ourselves, 'Who am I to be brilliant, gorgeous, talented, fabulous?' Actually, who are you not to be? You are a child of God. Your playing small does not serve the world. There is nothing enlightened about shrinking so that other people won't feel insecure around you. We are all meant to shine, as children do. We were born to make manifest the glory of God that is within us. It's not just in some of us; it's in everyone. And as we let our own light shine, we unconsciously give other people permission to do the same. As we are liberated from our own fear, our presence automatically liberates others.

Marianne Williamson, *A Return to Love*

Once the talking stick has made its way around the circle, and each woman and girl has had a chance to check-in, we move our attention to this evening's heroine. Through powerful and provocative discussion questions, we explore her life and honor her strengths and gifts.

Following this discussion, we pass around a small wicker basket containing slips of paper, each featuring a meaningful quote from our heroine. Like opening a fortune cookie or finding a message in a bottle from a faraway land, this ritual has the flavor of divination. Breaking into mother-daughter pairs, we share and discuss our selected quotes together. There is an excitement in the air: "Which one did you get? What do you think she meant by that? How might we apply her wisdom to our lives today?" After a few minutes, we check back in with the circle, sharing from our hearts what the gift of her words means for our lives and any connections that were made.

Each month's heroine offers us a special affirmation that we have been incorporating throughout the month at home with our daughters. We discuss this month's affirmation and then distribute the craft supplies to share a simple activity together, allowing our daughters to absorb this message in a hands-on, age-appropriate way. Once complete, each girl is eager to share her creation with the group and the mothers remark that they have learned something new about their daughters in the process of creating alongside them.

As our circle comes to an end, we take a conscious breath together, and are led through a short meditation, visualizing our heroine in all her glory. We are invited to speak words or phrases into the circle that summarize or describe her; words such as *brave, loyal, kind, strong, honest, determined, self-loving, beautiful, wise, compassionate*, and *confident* are spoken, and we are reminded that all the qualities she possessed also live within us. As heroine Dr. Elizabeth Blackwell once said, "What is done or learned by one class of women becomes, by virtue of their common womanhood, the property of all women." To symbolize this commonality, each mother-daughter pair then lights a small, individual candle from the larger candle that has been burning throughout our circle. With our faces bathed in the gentle warmth of candlelight, we sing our closing song together, followed by our empowering benediction:

May We Love Ourselves.
May We Love Each Other.
May We Believe that Our Dreams Can Come True.
We Are Strong.
We Are Wise.
We Are the Heroines of our Own Lives

As the candles are blown out, there is a palpable feeling of empowerment, inspiration, and love.

This, dear woman, is the magic of the Heroines Club.

In Part Two, I will offer you the complete curriculum and everything you need to know to share this magic with your own community. But first, let's consider the foundation of the Heroines Club.

THE POWER OF CONSCIOUS STORYTELLING

Storytelling is one of our oldest teaching tools and healing arts. Most historians and psychologists believe storytelling is one of the many elements that define and bind our humanity: humans are perhaps the only animals that create and tell stories. In fact, history itself is nothing but a series of stories that, when told correctly, can teach us lessons, offer us insights, and entertain us. Without our stories, we would not learn from our mistakes, would never dream to emulate past heroines, and would never see anything but the here and now. We have to know where we've been to know where we can go. Being ignorant of our past would leave us hopeless for our future. Storytelling is a powerful vehicle that persuades the listener in a way that our evolutionary history has primed our brains to receive.

Stories have to be told or they die, and when they die, we can't remember who we are or why we're here.

Sue Monk Kidd

Stories are ubiquitous and our daughters encounter stories every day, often without the awareness that they are an audience. One salient example of this unconscious storytelling is advertising. Companies hire marketing teams with psychology expertise and spend billions every year crafting their stories to influence us to buy their products or to think we need their services. These persuasive commercials can feel like an assault because most often the storyline they are promulgating is that we are lacking: we aren't good enough, smart enough, rich enough, thin enough, etc. Our supposed deficits continue *ad nauseam*. Storytelling is powerful, and advertisers know this.

Thankfully, as mothers, we can use the power of story to uplift our daughters. The Heroines Club is built on the foundation that our girls are listening and we have a unique access to their developing selves through conscious storytelling.

Conscious storytelling is the intentional use of story to educate, empower, comfort, and guide. Through conscious storytelling, we have the powerful opportunity to reach our daughters in a way they are open to receiving. Knowing this, we set the intention to offer them empowering female narratives, both from our own lives and lineage, and from other remarkable women in history. Over time, these stories create a feathered nest where a girl knows she belongs, and from which she can fly, knowing it is a safe place for her to always return.

So, what stories do our daughters need most as they travel the path from little girls to young women?

Stories of the women from which she comes

As a young girl, I felt a magnetic pull whenever my mother and her sister friends gathered in conversation. I could not keep my eyes off of them! When their conversation would shift to a hushed tone or after a sidelong glance in my direction, my whole little girl being would perk up and tune in like a radio antenna, straining to catch any morsel of the story. I was subconsciously taking notes—learning from women what it meant to be a woman. Now, as a mother, I see this same hunger in my daughter. She yearns to be near me, to be privy to the stories being told between Aunt Lindsay and Mom in the front seat of the minivan, just beyond earshot. Like a detective keenly searching for clues, our daughters are solving the mystery of womanhood itself.

A 2010 study from Emory University's Center for Myth and Ritual in American Life found a link between family knowledge and emotional well-being in children. In this study, the researchers used a twenty-question family knowledge scale alongside multiple standardized measures of family functioning, identity development, and well-being. They concluded that when children know more about their family's history, they enjoy a stronger sense of control over their lives, higher self-esteem, and a belief that their families functioned successfully. There is power in knowing the stories from where we come. Recognizing and honoring the dignity, strength and accomplishments of the women in our own families leads to higher self-esteem in our daughters. Hearing stories about their mothers, grandmothers, and great-grandmothers helps our daughters to better understand their lives, the challenges they faced and ultimately better understand themselves. When stories like these are passed down from one generation to the next, we keep the present in touch with the past, reaffirm values and pass on wisdom.

By design, the Heroines Club offers us the structure and opportunity for these empowering stories to be told. Daughters sit on the edges of their seats, with sparkling, unblinking eyes as their mothers respond to check-in questions and discussion prompts, such as "when was a time that you felt afraid, but chose to act with courage?" and "what dreams did you have for yourself when you were a little girl?" Through conscious storytelling, we capture our daughters' attention and contribute to their overall sense of well-being.

What about adopted and blended families?

There are many types of family situations, including adoption and blended families. The Heroines Club is absolutely appropriate for all family configurations. The stories of family history we share with our daughters in circle need not be genetic in origin; all children in a family have equal ownership to the family history because family is based on mutual love, connection, and sacrifice—not chromosomes.

Stories of real-life heroines

In a spiritual sense, we are all related and interconnected and any act of wisdom, courage, compassion or grace by one woman belongs to all women. Knowing the stories of history's real-life heroic women offers your daughter comfort and inspiration as she faces inevitable challenges and hardships in her own life. Unfortunately, chances are your daughter will spend a disproportionate amount of time in school studying the men who shaped their country (and the world at large.) Although some respectable attempts have been made to correct this imbalance in the U.S., since the introduction of Title 9, which prohibited "sex discrimination against students and employees of educational institutions" in the 1970s, textbooks and classroom lessons today still fall short of a complete and equally represented history. Dr. Myra Pollack Sadker pioneered much of the research documenting gender bias in American schools. In her book, *Failing at Fairness: How America's Schools Cheat Girls,* Sadker shares that a history text for sixth graders, published in 1992, only mentioned eleven female names! Sadker and colleagues conducted a research experiment in which people were asked to list famous women from history, the only limitation being that they could not name entertainers or president's wives. How do you think people did? How would your daughter do? Too often, the lists only contained a few names or none at all.

Dr. Alan Ravitz, a prominent child and adolescent psychiatrist at the Child Mind Institute in New York City, explains that, "as kids individualize themselves from their parents, which is a natural part of development and growing up, they try to establish psychological and emotional independence. No matter the culture, they need somebody to look to, aside from their parents, for guidance and a model for becoming an adult." Considering the lack of women's history and real-life role models offered in our school curriculums, to whom are our daughters turning to meet their developmental (and universal) need for role models? Culture icons and the influence of advertising are not sufficient substitutes. Young girls wearing Taylor Swift or Miley Cyrus t-shirts, engrossed in the latest YouTube videos, need role models with a more lasting and positive impact. Sure, we did it as children too—Madonna and Kylie Minogue graced many of our childhood bedroom walls—but what exactly did these teen idols offer us and what are they offering our daughters? Celebrity worship and an obsession with teen idols can result in lost self-esteem in children, and this loss of self-esteem can lead to poor family relationships, poor body image, and even eating disorders. Dr. Lin Fang, assistant professor in the faculty of social work at the University of Toronto cautions parents of adolescent girls against the common, but not actually harmless, idolization of pop stars:

Research shows that girls who strongly idolize celebrities tend to buy into other aspects of commercial culture and may become overly materialistic. The pressure coming from celebrities with perfect bodies may lead to an unrealistic body image and possibly nurture eating disorders, which can consume a child's life.

With awareness and intention, we can leverage this innate desire for role models and provide healthy examples for our daughters to emulate. By reading this book and participating in the Heroines Club with your daughter, you will provide her an abundance of strong women with whom she can choose to identify. When introduced in the fun, communal nature of the Heroines Club, women such as Joan of Arc and Ruby Bridges can truly meet girls' developmental need for role models.

In some countries around the world, March is designated as Women's History Month, highlighting the contributions of women to historical events and contemporary society. Every year at this time, schools focus on a handful of well-known, front-runner women-in-history. While this is progress, at the Heroines Club, we believe that our daughters deserve more than one month a year and we know there are incalculable women worth recognizing who are currently overlooked within our current educational syllabi.

Heroines are Human

By definition, a heroine is a woman admired or idealized for her courage, outstanding achievements, or noble qualities. The heroines represented in this curriculum are all women who overcame their own difficulties and the restrictions of their own cultures to achieve great things in the world. They are women worthy of our daughters' admiration and emulation.

But I want to be very clear here: they are also just real people, and as we know, real people are flawed. The heroines, while incredibly inspirational, are not infallible, above criticism, beyond reproach, or without controversy. None of us is. The fact that they stepped forth to be the powerful, visible, pioneering women they were called to be—even with their imperfections—is part of what makes them true heroines.

There is tremendous cultural pressure placed on girls and women to succeed—nay, to be *perfect*—in every domain. While the Western sociological concept of "superwoman" that evolved in the 1980s has been used as a term of empowerment, we could also consider it a form of backlash. We live in a culture that tells women in myriad ways, "you must not step out in your power unless you are perfect and beyond reproach and unless you please all the people all the time." This pressure causes many of our brilliant sisters to feel the need to "wait" until they have it all together—until they are thin enough, rich enough, credentialed enough, healed enough, whatever enough—to begin offering their divine gifts and medicine to the world. The superwoman identity—having it all, doing it all, pleasing all—is, for most healthy humans, unattainable. The twelve heroic women represented in these pages offer us an important message: you don't have to be perfect to be a heroine.

Therefore, just as in real-life relationships, you may find that you like, or resonate with, one heroine more than others, or you may not agree with all the details of a particular heroine's life or world view. I encourage you to take what works and leave the rest. Just as in circle, everyone is welcome and there is space for every loving path.

Well behaved women seldom make history.

Laurel Thatcher Ulrich

EMPOWERING MOTHERS & DAUGHTERS, TOGETHER

More than Girl Power

These are potent times to be alive on the planet. We are mothering our daughters in the dynamic and hopeful era of third-wave feminism. Having reaped the hard-earned benefits of the first wave (suffrage and expanded opportunities in the first decades of the twentieth century), as well as the second wave (sexuality and reproductive rights in the 1970s and 1980s), the girls of the third wave are stepping onto the stage strong and empowered, eschewing victimization and defining feminine beauty for themselves. This is what we most want for our daughters and indeed for ourselves: to be the strong and empowered heroines of our own lives. In the last twenty-five years or so, our culture has mirrored this swelling of third-wave feminism most notably in the marketplace; we see this in our everyday lives by the presence of what are often referred to as "girl power" toys, clothing, media and extracurricular opportunities. An example is the recent rise in "girl power" camps, workshops, and

Attend me, hold me in your strong, flowering arms, and protect me from throwing any parts of myself away.

Audre Lorde

after-school classes being offered in many communities, designed to encourage girls to embrace the full complement of their talents and strengths through messages of self-esteem and sovereignty— messages that those of us born just one generation earlier, for the most part, did not receive.

I have such gratitude and respect for these offerings and their important message which is in powerful alignment with the core themes of the Heroines Club curriculum. What makes the Heroines Club so unique and transformative is that the empowering messages the girls receive are coming from the lips of their first and most powerful teachers—their own mothers. While empowering girls themselves is a step in the right direction, empowering mothers and daughters together takes us right to the heart of the legacy we wish to create for all women.

Although the curriculum offered in these pages could be adapted for use in a girls-only camp or workshop, by including the mothers, the impact of the experience for our daughters grows tremendously. If our goal is a true and lasting empowerment, it is my stalwart belief that we must serve mothers and daughters alongside each other. In doing so, the benefits will reverberate throughout our lifetimes, like the waves from a pebble thrown into a pond.

The Unmatched Influence of Mother

We are our mothers' daughters. When I was a little girl my voice echoed my mother's so closely that when I answered our home telephone, nearly every caller thought I was my mother. At age fourteen, the notion that my mother had somehow set up shop in my head and mouth drove me bonkers! As you might expect, as an adult I now take pride in being mistaken for my mother.

From the time we are born, our mothers are models of what it means to be a woman, and for better or worse, their imprint dwells forever in our psyches. I see this impact routinely in my work as a transformational life coach. My clients always bring another person to every discussion—their mothers. In her book, *Mother-Daughter Wisdom: Understanding the Crucial Link Between Mothers, Daughters, and Health*, Christiane Northrup, M.D. writes,

> *No other childhood experience is as compelling as a young girl's relationship with her mother. Each of us takes in at the cellular level how our mother feels about being female, what she believes about her body, how she takes care of her health, and what she believes is possible in her life. Her beliefs and behaviors set the tone for how well we learn to care for ourselves as adults.*

We mothers have a wonderfully precious and truly powerful role to play in the future self-images of our daughters. The truth is, the most effective way to inculcate in our daughters a fighting chance at life-long self-love and empowerment is not in the books we read to them, or the workshops we send them to, or the media we do or do not expose them to, or even the things we tell them, rather it is in the reflection of self-love and empowerment they see in us, their mothers. The model of our own empowerment gives our daughters permission to be powerful. Of course, culture and societal norms mold our view of ourselves as women, but the beliefs and behaviors of our mothers are far more influential.

And this is good news! For though we cannot always control our daughter's life experiences within the context of modern culture, we can control the model she receives from her mother, and our model will triumph every time. Carol Gilligan, a pre-eminent voice in feminist studies and the founder of the Harvard Center for Gender and Education, has said that "a girl's valuing of herself is stunted when it's not joined and strengthened by the mother." In other words, if a mother does not value and protect certain qualities in herself, such as a positive body image and good physical and mental

A mother who radiates self-love and self-acceptance actually vaccinates her daughter against low self-esteem.

Naomi Wolf

health, it will be difficult for her daughter to value and protect them in herself.

The Dance of Mother Guilt

The truth is, we cannot give to our daughters what we ourselves do not yet have. In this journey of mothering empowered daughters, we cannot skip ourselves. That is not how true generational healing and change works.

Hearing this, many of us may feel fear or guilt in the face of our past shortcomings and the seemingly vast distance between where we are now and where we want to be. What I really want to say is that these feelings are natural and it is never too late to begin. As heroine and mother Dr. Maya Angelou once wrote, "I did then what I knew how to do. Now that I know better, I do better." If the idea of communicating and modeling your own self-love and empowerment feels new and foreign to you, know that this curriculum is specifically designed to support you in that process. We are all (re)learning to love ourselves and we are all in this together.

The "dance" of mother guilt and blame is epidemic in our society. By releasing ourselves from this patriarchal prison, we end what have been dubbed the "mommy wars," we strengthen our relationships with our daughters, and we offer ourselves the unconditional compassion and grace we so deserve. We do not have to be fretfully concerned with our every move as mothers, rather it is the big picture—the ongoing nature of how and what we communicate—that is paramount. Of course we will fail our daughters at times. We are human. I truly believe that our occasional shortcomings are not only tolerable, but that they are likely part of the grand plan for our daughters' life journey in some unseen way. In the face of my own personal imperfections and the nuanced generational wounds from which I am continuously healing, I find comfort in knowing that I am guided by my desire to transform the legacy my daughter will inherit.

I encourage you to view this curriculum as a path toward real empowerment, not just for your daughter, but also for you. Each month, place a picture of the honoree heroine somewhere you will see often, incorporate the affirmation into your daily practices, and get to know these powerful women. I promise that if you are open to it, their messages and medicine will transform you alongside your daughter. Dear woman, your influence is unmatched and your healing is worth fighting for.

Mothers and Daughters Together

Have you ever wondered why the plot of most Disney movies includes the death of the heroine's mother? The Little Mermaid's mother? Killed by pirates. Snow White? "And when she was born, the queen died." Even when mom is not abruptly killed off, she is missing in action. Did Sleeping Beauty or Belle even have mothers? In fiction, it seems mothers are only good for giving birth, and then they must immediately exit stage left.

Kieth Merrill, an Academy Award-winning director, says there is a reason we rarely find strong mothers in movies today. "If you're a screenwriter, and you understand drama, and you want to plunge your characters into conflict, you have to 'lose the mom.' Mothers go missing in movies because leaving them in the lives of characters in crisis makes sustaining conflict difficult," he says.

Indeed, mothers and daughters together are a powerful force to be reckoned with. Would the storyline of Cinderella still work with a strong and loving mother involved? Would Jasmine have sought adventure and romance outside the palace walls with a mother present? Media and culture tell our girls that they cannot have a mother without thwarting their adventures, and thus the storyline.

At the Heroines Club, we know that in this instance at least, life does not have to imitate art: mothers and daughters can be the heroines of their own lives, together. Rather than stymieing our daughters, we are leading the way, breaking the glass ceilings and making room for them to stand strong next to us.

The sacred time you set aside with your daughter for the Heroines Club is not just another item on your to-do list (goodness knows we have enough already!), but rather it is an investment. The focused time and energy spent connecting and having fun together actually makes mothering our daughters easier, as all aspects of parenting flow much more smoothly when the relationship is healthy and strong. We have likely all heard of the reassuring research in recent years demonstrating that quality time with our children trumps the amount of time spent together with regard to long-term effects on academic achievement, and behavioral and emotional well-being.

So, what exactly is quality time? Quality time is time devoted to being with your daughter together, offering her your whole-hearted attention, and engaging in activities you both enjoy, in order to strengthen the relationship. Quality time is a powerful emotional communicator of love. As Dr Anthony P. Whitman said, "Children spell love . . . T – I – M – E."

Many things happen throughout our daughters' lives that they need to talk about, and by spending quality time with them, we give them the comfort level and opportunity to share these things with us. Regardless of your parenting philosophy, your daughter needs to spend meaningful time with you, individually. In families with more than one child in the home, consciously carving out this time is especially important, as families typically have a group dynamic that differs significantly from the one-on-one experience. Quality time alone with each child offers us a chance to get to know them as individuals, and gives them the opportunity to speak with us and share what is in their heart, unencumbered. By participating in the Heroines Club, you are giving yourself the permission—and the nourishing structure—to ensure quality time with your daughter is guaranteed. In fact, above all else that the Heroines Club offers, the simple and far-reaching gift of quality time is likely the most tangible reward.

The Heroines Club Community

By reading this book, you are already joining arms with a global community of mothers who want to proactively shape their daughters' sense of self, and to nurture the most fundamental relationships in her life: the relationship with herself and the relationship with her mother. While this program is extremely powerful to share alone with your daughter, I encourage you to find (or create) an on-the-ground circle of other like-minded mothers and daughters with whom to share the journey.

It takes a whole village to raise a child.

African proverb

When our daughters were babies and preschoolers, we had built-in opportunities for connection with other mothers through play-dates, playgroups, preschool pick-up, La Leche League meetings or other mother/baby support groups. By elementary school, these opportunities are diminishing, but our need for a supportive community is ever present. In the chapter *Everything You Need to Know . . .* , I will show you how to build your own Heroines Club with other mothers who share similar concerns and values, and whose parenting style is to talk openly and directly about the passages our girls navigate on their journey to womanhood. On this journey, the impact of positive peer influences and a conscious community of other women cannot be understated. Our daughters, like climbing vines, will thrive with the guiding trellis of the Heroines Club community, training them to grow in an optimal direction. This level of thriving simply cannot happen without the power of mothers and daughters, together.

For your further inspiration ...

Mother Daughter Revolution: From Good Girls to Great Women, by Debold, E.

Altered Loves: Mothers and Daughters During Adolescence, by Apter, T.

AN INTRODUCTION TO SACRED MOTHER-DAUGHTER CIRCLING

A circle, the only geometric shape defined by its center, is a sacred symbol honored throughout time to represent limitless possibilities—love with no beginning and no end. Throughout the ages, women from all walks of life, religions, belief systems, and cultures have been gathering in sacred circles to co-create community and share in the abundance of women's wisdom. History tells us that from primitive times onward, women have gathered to collaborate, vision, and discuss together, and that these gatherings have, more often than not, taken the shape of a circle. As psychiatrist, Jungian analyst, author, and leader in the women's empowerment movement, Dr. Jean Shinoda Bolen, has said, "Circles are the means through which women have improved the situation for women."

Today, circles with a sacred center are (re)forming everywhere, and there is a re-awakening of this ancient vessel for personal, and thus global, evolution. Women are gathering in circles of support for each other in healing circles, wisdom circles, soul sister circles, circles of wise women, of community mothers, of grandmothers. Even in the business place and in cyberspace, women are re-claiming the circle

Life is a full circle, widening until it joins the circle motions of the infinite.

Anaïs Nin

with a spiritual center as their own. We are doing this because, deep in our bones, we know it feels right to be supported in a community of other women. We sense this is the familiar medicine of our most venerable great-grandmothers, lovingly preserved for us since time immemorial as the key to our personal fulfillment and collective well-being.

As I shared in the Introduction, sacred circling with other women changed my life and propelled me to bring the healing practice of circling to one of life's most complex relationships—that of mothers and daughters. Like us, our daughters need the medicine of women circling together to reach their full potential, and they need not wait until they are adults themselves to receive it. The Heroines Club, created with all the essential elements of a sacred circle, offers mothers a developmentally appropriate way to give their daughters the gifts of circling and community.

What is a Sacred Circle? The Key Ingredients

On the surface, a sacred circle of women looks simply like a group of sisters, gathered in a living room or other discrete place, to discuss a shared topic. On the surface there is talking, listening, laughing. But look closer and there's crying, witnessing, mirroring, deepening, role-modeling, grieving, drawing upon experience, and sharing the wisdom of experience. And then, below the surface of all of that goodness lie even more riches: a swell of healing, blessing and unmistakable transformation occurs.

There are some fundamental, key ingredients required for any sacred circle to be healthy and effective. The Heroines Club is based on these crucial components, and it is important that you keep these intentions at the forefront of your heart as you develop and maintain your own successful Heroines Club.

The following eight principles of sacred circling create the unique experience that mothers and daughters share together at the Heroines Club:

Sanctity

Circle time is meant to be sacred. As we enter circle, we step away from our everyday routine and enter a place of healing, blessing and replenishing. There is an agreement, both spoken and unspoken, to hold each other and the gathering itself as sacred. Even the youngest of daughters will recognize and appreciate the reverent aspects of circling. When we enter circle, we come with love, consciousness, honor, and respect, setting the intention for a soulful, bonding, and heart-opening experience.

Safety

Trust is paramount. For deep sharing, learning, and personal growth to germinate, mothers and daughters must know that their expressions are safe and will be protected with the strictest confidence. In circle, we trust that our personal stories will be kept confidential. While we are certainly encouraged to talk about our own experiences in circle, we do not share the words, information, or stories of another mother or daughter with anyone outside of the circle.

The circle is everyday ceremony: the invention of our most ancient godmothers, who, upon witnessing the myriad ways nature exalted this humble shape, claimed it as the spiritual center of their communities. Held by the simple rituals of opening and completion, honoring and appreciation, the circle acts as a vehicle for both storytelling and transcending our stories. In circle, we are conversing with the Divine.

Baraka Elihu

Witnessing

Bearing witness is a sacred act and a profound honor. Witnessing between women deepens and fortifies the soul of both the woman sharing and the woman bearing witness. To be a sacred witness means to simply hold space for what is. In concrete terms, this means that when a mother or daughter shares a check-in or responds to a discussion question, we listen with our full heart and mind; we give her our full attention. When she finishes speaking, we do not respond with any cross talk, advice, fixing, "what I would do is," referrals, or feedback. With acceptance and honor we simply say, "Thank you for sharing your heart/wisdom/experience/story/ thoughts with us." We offer gratitude for her process, trusting that each woman (and girl) already has all the answers she needs within herself and that, like a flower growing toward the sunlight, she naturally bends toward healing. We do not have to "do" anything to affect positive change in our sisters' lives; as quantum physics teaches us, the simple (and profound) act of observation can literally change reality. Listening is loving.

Authenticity

On the stone pathway to the gathering place of the original Heroines Club at the Mother-Daughter Nest rests a sign that reads: "Just show up." Authenticity is letting what we are experiencing on the inside "show up" on the outside. Authenticity is courageously uncovering and expressing how we deeply feel. Our deeper, tender feelings are a large part of what makes us human, and circle holds space for this authentic sharing. In circle, we practice pausing, going inside, taking a breath and noticing how we feel in our body before we speak, so we are more likely to find words that reflect an earnestness that connects us in a more fulfilling way to ourselves and others. Circle says, "come, show up and be exactly who you are, exactly where you are in your life, at this very moment." Feeling the unconditional love and acceptance of circle, mothers and daughters feel safe enough to remove any social masks and remember the beautiful truth of who they really are.

Silence

Silence has energy to it like no other source. By recognizing the silences within our circle discussion and embracing those soft spaces, we connect more deeply with ourselves. In circle, silence is valued for allowing us to digest what was said and discover what will be given voice to next as it emerges in the present moment. Silence offers an opportunity to unearth the mysteries and lessons that exist within and allows for individuals to integrate their experience, staying grounded and engaged. When a woman or girl honors the voice of her silence and the power to not speak by "passing" the talking stick, we thank her in the same manner as when she shares from her heart with words. Welcoming silence requires practice because many of us instinctively feel uneasy when encountering pauses or interruptions in flow and we often feel an impetus to fill the perceived void. In circle, we know this is not necessary and we resist the habit of filling silent gaps with superficial talk. Silence, as the old saying goes, is indeed, golden.

Ritual

A sacred circle includes some form of ritual. For many people today, the idea of ritual is associated with exotic religions or the occult. Others may believe that rituals are something only ordained priests or ministers can access and create. The truth is anyone—from any religious path or belief system or none—can participate in and benefit from the act of ritual. Ritual is simply any action taken with the intention to remember our connection to the Divine (God, Goddess, Highest Self, etc.) and the grand plan of Life. At the Heroines Club, a simple candlelight ritual, which will be described in the chapter *Implementing the Curriculum*, carries the circle into the sacred realm, potentiating and elevating the experience for all.

Co-Creation

Just as we co-create our experience of life, we co-create our experience of circle. There is no hierarchy in circle and all participants including one or two facilitators have a precisely equal role in the process. Circle allows that everyone and every expression within the circle is equal. Each circle co-creates its own powerful synergy, which would not be possible without each woman's specific participation and unique offerings. As we say in the Heroines Club, "We are all the teachers, and we are all the taught."

Conscious Community Building

The Heroines Club creates a circuit of energy with other mothers that magnifies the love, nurturing, grace, and empowerment we offer our daughters. From this experience, a community is born based in love and support, giving and receiving. Belonging to this conscious community of other mothers and daughters offers a sense of identity, helping us understand who we are and knowing we are a part of something larger than ourselves.

In the chapter *Implementing the Curriculum*, I will apply these elements of sacred circling to the Heroines Club curriculum. If you would like to deepen your journey, the following resources offer information and inspiration on women's sacred circles:

Birthing Ourselves into Being, by Elihu, B. and Weaver, A. (Fall 2016, Womancraft Publishing)

The Millionth Circle: How to Change Ourselves and the World – the Essential Guide to Women's Circles, by Shinoda Bolen, J.

Sacred Circles: A Guide to Creating Your Own Women's Spirituality Group, by Deen Carnes, R. and Craig, S.

Circle of Stones: Woman's Journey to Herself, by Duerk, J.

EVERYTHING YOU NEED TO KNOW . . .
to set up your club and keep it strong

Setting Up Your Circle

The previous chapters have laid the foundation on which to build your club. Now we will consider the framework and structures needed to keep your club strong and enduring. Whether you are envisioning an intimate gathering of just a couple of other mothers and daughters or are planning to bring the gift of the Heroines Club to your larger community, building and sustaining a successful Heroines Club requires some conscious planning. Here are the most important questions you will want to consider before your first circle ever meets.

Groups run by women are our psychic turf, our place to discover who we are, or who we could become, as whole independent beings. Somewhere in our lives, each of us needs a free place—a little psychic territory. Do you have yours?

Gloria Steinem

Who will lead?

In the methodology of the Heroines Club, there are one or two dedicated facilitators planning and guiding the circle. However, if a group of mothers wants to share the responsibility, facilitation duties can be rotated among members, or shared in some other way, as long as everyone is committed. Being an effective facilitator is a skill and an art, and a role for which any woman is qualified, should she feel called.

The responsibility of the facilitator is to: plan and prepare for the circle (using the curriculum as your guide), create an environment where participants can flourish, and guide discussions to maintain focus and depth, while honoring both the flow of the group and the time boundaries.

Who will be invited?

Time and again, it has been my experience that the people who are meant for this kind of work are the ones drawn to it, and each mother and daughter who chooses to participate is there for a reason. With this in mind, choosing whom to invite is an important consideration as the health and longevity of your circle is largely determined by the cohesion of the circle as a whole. Diversity of race, religion, socio-economic status, and so forth is desirable, as people with different backgrounds, skills, attitudes and experiences will bring fresh ideas and perceptions. What is essential is that despite those differences, all of the mothers are united in their vision for the circle. Of utmost importance is that the mothers share similar values and are in accordance about the purpose of the Heroines Club.

It is easier to discuss issues—both logistical and philosophical—and to know what the Heroines Club journey will entail, when all mothers have the same information for their foundation. For this reason, each mother should read at least Part One of this book before committing to joining the circle. Having this as a pre-requisite for participation will ensure a good fit between mothers, while providing a strong base of shared knowledge and inspiration for those women who will be joining your circle.

What will be the age-range of daughters?

The Heroines Club circles that I facilitate at The Mother-Daughter Nest in Athens, Georgia are divided into two age groups, lovingly referred to as "Little Sisters" and "Big Sisters." The Little Sisters circle is for girls age seven to ten and the Big Sisters circle is for girls age eleven to fourteen. Having a mixed age-range of a few years optimizes the educative potential for all, as the younger girls learn from the older girls, and the older girls have an opportunity to strengthen their leadership skills.

Of course, the needs of mothers and daughters and the nature of the discussions evolve as girls grow and mature. Therefore, it is not recommended to have an age-range larger than a few years.

What is an ideal circle size?

Since the Heroines Club explores personal issues and matters of the heart, a smaller, more intimate circle is best. From experience, I have found that a circle of three to five pairs (six to ten people) is just right. This number of participants is enough to stimulate discussion, but not so many as to intimidate quieter members, or compromise privacy or emotional safety.

What will be the investment from the participants?

The Heroines Club is not a "for-profit" venture; instead we aim that each member feels her investment is met with equal return, so that all may benefit together.

The investments required to implement a successful Heroines

Club circle include:

◎ To plan for each monthly circle using the curriculum as your guide.

◎ To buy, gather, create, and prepare the needed supplies for each monthly circle.

◎ To prepare the space before, and to clean the space after, each monthly circle.

◎ To implement the curriculum and facilitate the circle through an empowering, bonding, and heart-opening experience.

◎ To purchase Integrated Activity supplies.

◎ To purchase snacks and refreshments (if desired.)

◎ To purchase ritual candles, attendance log book, and talking stick (if desired.)

The total investment of time, energy, and financial costs associated with the Heroines Club should be factored into the overall exchange among members and explicitly agreed upon ahead of time. There are many creative ways to address the investment among participants. For the health and longevity of your circle, it is absolutely necessary to give this careful thought and to be clear on this from the beginning.

The financial cost associated with providing the supplies needed for the monthly Integrated Activities ranges from $250–$350 total for the year, depending on what supplies you already have on hand, and the number of participants in your circle. An equitable approach is to divide that amount by the number of participants, and require each member to contribute a "supply fee" prior to beginning the circle, which the facilitator will use solely for the purchasing of supplies.

In addition to the financial investment for supplies, the amount of time, energy, and attention the facilitator is offering the circle must be compensated in some way, so as not to create a situation that breeds exhaustion, burnout, or resentment. For the health of your circle, the facilitator should create healthy boundaries and expectations to ensure that she is not doing it all with little return. The facilitator needs to receive energy, in order to give of her energy fully without experiencing burnout. This can be accomplished by dividing tasks and responsibilities among mothers, charging a small additional fee to compensate the facilitator for her time and energy, or bartering with the facilitator in some fashion. **I cannot emphasize the importance of this enough.** For many of us, this will be challenging because it can feel incredibly uncomfortable to ask for money to do the things we are good at doing, want to do, or enjoy doing—especially if it involves close friends.

There is no right or wrong way to address the investment among participants. The way I have chosen to do it as creator and facilitator of the Heroines Club is to charge $25 per circle, which comes to $300 per year, per mother-daughter pair. In return for this financial investment, mothers and daughters have no additional responsibilities other than to show up and receive.

Each circle will be unique, and what feels good and right for one, may not for another. I encourage you to practice sovereignty in deciding what feels good and fair for you and your circle. Finally, a truth I have learned is this: others will only value our time and energy if we demonstrate that we value our time and energy.

Where will your circle gather?

The container for your circle sets the tone for the experience. The meeting space should feel special, cozy, and safe. I recommend meeting in a private office space or in members' homes. Above all, the space you choose should feel physically comfortable and allow for close connection, while protecting the circle from any outside intrusion or unnecessary distractions.

What will be the frequency and duration of circle gatherings?

The Heroines Club curriculum is designed to be a once-a-month gathering, spanning over the course of one year. However, some circles may choose to take off the summer or holiday months to allow for travel and other plans. Different circles will have different preferences and the curriculum can be adapted to meet various schedule needs and desires.

The duration of the circle, given all of its elements, can last anywhere from one and a half to two hours. It is crucial to the health of the circle that whatever time boundaries are decided on are consistently honored. This means that circle members trust that circle will start on time and end on time. To ensure this happens, I recommend explicitly stating and agreeing with the mothers ahead of time that each circle will begin and end at the designated times. If a member arrives late to circle, they are invited to quietly enter and take their seats in the already in progress circle. Periodically throughout the circle, the facilitator will check the time to ensure that the rhythm and pace is on track, making adjustments as needed, to honor the agreed upon end time.

Keeping Your Circle Healthy and Strong

There are some common growing pains that your club may encounter, and by anticipating and communicating about them, your club will remain healthy, strong, and sustainable. I recommend the following measures to prevent circle deterioration and to maintain overall enthusiasm and goodwill.

Mothers-only organizational and intention-setting circle

Prior to your first Heroines Club circle, hold an organizational and intention-setting circle for the mothers. This will allow time for mothers to meet one another, discuss the expectations for circle participation, set and share intentions for what each mother hopes to gain from this experience with her daughter, and also have the opportunity to share anything they would like the circle to know about them or about their daughter. The initial mothers-only circle is extremely powerful and special. It generates excitement for the upcoming year, and establishes a bond between the mothers that will continue to strengthen with each circle.

Review the "commitments" at every circle

The Heroines Club rules will be explained in detail in Part Two. It is helpful to open every circle with a reading of the rules to serve as a reminder of the agreed upon commitments.

Periodic "health of the circle" check-ins

Seasonally, either in person or online, the facilitator will hold space for any sharing and reflection regarding the health of the circle as a whole.

◎　How are the commitments being honored?

◎　How is the circle as a whole serving the members?

◎　Is there anything that needs to be addressed?

◎　Is there anything not working anymore?

Even if things are running smoothly, this preventative measure will promote group cohesion and ensure continued vitality.

Maintaining connection between circles

One of the greatest benefits of the Heroines Club is the supportive community and loving relationships that are created among members. When you close your monthly circle with the benediction, the circle is open, but it is never broken: members will maintain a loving energetic connection with one another throughout the month. This connection can be supported by making contact with one another, either through social gatherings or online. The Heroines Club that I facilitate has a private online Facebook group where mothers can check-in with one another, share inspiration and seek support throughout the month. There are many creative ways that your circle can maintain connection between circle gatherings, and it is a worthwhile endeavor to cultivate this connection in ways that feel supportive to all.

When someone leaves the circle

No matter how committed everyone is at the beginning, lives and circumstances change and sometimes even the most committed club will lose a mother-daughter pair along the way.

The Heroines Club circle is co-created among all members: each mother-daughter pair brings something special to the circle that would not exist without their presence. Like a hanging mobile, when one part changes or is moved, the other pieces are also affected. When this happens, it is helpful to honor the change with a simple ritual to acknowledge the circle's evolution and to lovingly release the departing mother and daughter from the circle.

The bonds formed between circle members strengthen over the course of the year, and the understanding of how the circle "works" is learned together as the year progresses. Therefore, depending on when a membership change occurs, it may or may not feel appropriate to replace lost members. As with everything, let your heart and intuition be your guide.

Dealing with conflict between members

The Heroines Club is a very intimate experience, and there are no substantive human relationships that are completely devoid of conflict. In fact, conflict can be healthy as every person in our lives acts as a mirror for us, reflecting parts of ourselves back to us, and offering us an opportunity to grow. In her book, *Calling the Circle*, Christian Baldwin recommends considering the following questions if you find yourself feeling provoked or thinking negatively about another circle member:

◎ How have I been pulled off center?

◎ What's my body telling me?

◎ What's my mind telling my body?

◎ Whose shadow work is this? And how do I own my piece with integrity?

◎ Who does this person remind me of?

◎ Am I seeing this situation through a filter of a past memory? Of judgment? Of fear?

After considering these questions, if the matter remains an issue, open and honest communication among members may be needed. In my experience, the Heroines Club has had very little serious conflict, perhaps from luck or perhaps due to the personalities of the members that are drawn to this work. Regardless, if your circle experiences conflict, it is best to approach it in an authentic, heart-centered way, allowing each member to share their thoughts and feelings, while owning their experience and speaking from the "I" place.

Honoring the circle's end

At the end of the twelve-month journey together, your Heroines Club circle will have shared a beautiful experience that will always be remembered and cherished. Just as you close circle each month with a ritual and benediction, you will mark and honor the circle's completion in some special way to provide space for reflection and closure. There are many ways to accomplish a meaningful end.

At the end of every year's Heroines Club, I like to hold a pot-luck meal. During this shared meal, we discuss questions, such as, "Who was your favorite heroine we got to know? What will you always remember about the Heroines Club? What did you enjoy most? What are you grateful for about this experience with your mother/daughter?"

At the end of the meal, we do a sweet ritual called the Sacred Give-Away, that I learned from an elder in my community. Each participant brings a gift from their "world" that has been meaningful in some way and reflects the journey they have experienced in circle this year. This is not a gift that is bought, but rather something which you already have and feel it is time for another person to own. I have seen rocks, feathers, scarves, paintings, books, candles, jewelry, household items, decorations and even a telescope brought as a sacred gift. It is not the monetary value of the item that counts, but rather the intention behind the gift and what it represents. Have each person place their unwrapped gift on the center altar and decide who will go first (we usually like to pick a number between one and twenty.) Whomever is chosen to go first then goes to the altar and chooses the gift that calls to them. They will say, "I believe this is my gift" and share why they chose it. They then ask, "Who brought me this gift?" At that point, the person who brought the gift will let themselves be known and tell the story of the object and what it represents to them. It is then the giver's turn to receive a gift from the altar. And so it goes until all the gifts are given and each person has a special reminder of the magic that was made together that year.

IMPLEMENTING THE HEROINES CLUB CURRICULUM
Creating Your Own Magic

Part Two of this book offers twelve complete circle templates to see you through one full year of facilitating your very own Heroines Club. Here, we will explore in detail how to implement those monthly templates to offer the mothers and daughters of your community a positive, heart-opening and bonding experience.

Are you ready to make your own Heroines Club magic? The first thing to consider is how to prepare the environment to set the tone for your sacred mother-daughter circle.

Preparing the Environment

The space that the mothers and daughters first walk into sets the tone for the circle and speaks to the expectations of circle behavior without saying a word. Mothers and daughters instinctively know they are stepping into a place of reverence, safety, self-exploration and mother-daughter bonding by the way the room is arranged, organized, and decorated. Consider these elements when preparing the space for your Heroines Club gathering:

Seating

Sitting in a sacred mother-daughter circle entails—you guessed it—sitting in a circle! The circular seating arrangement reflects the egalitarian nature of the Heroines Club, while encouraging discussion and familiarity. Seating should be physically comfortable and promote mother-daughter bonding. Couches are great for this, as well as floor cushions and pillows. Mothers and daughters should be invited and encouraged to sit beside one another.

Lighting

Lighting sets the mood. Our bodies respond energetically to the color and intensity of the light around us, and our emotions respond accordingly. There is a reason why most fancy, romantic restaurants keep the lighting low and provide candlelight: low, warm lighting promotes relaxation and intimacy, and aids in the release of oxytocin, a key hormone for bonding. Consider turning off overhead lights, and gently illuminating the space with lamps and candlelight.

Altar

Altars have been used for thousands of years as a place to express creativity, tap into intuition, reflect on the things of personal importance and value, and connect with the Divine of your understanding. We all create altars, whether we realize it or not. For example, most of us have special places in our homes where we put family photos, special mementos, and natural items we cherish. Your

Heroines Club altar is a physical representation of your intentions for the circle and it serves as a beautifully designed place for the eyes to gaze throughout circle. Place a coffee table or other small table to serve as an altar in the center of your circle. If you are all sitting on the floor, you may wish to use a special quilt or cloth for this purpose so as to have the altar at everyone's eye level. On the altar, place a framed photograph of that month's honoree heroine. These can be purchased online, or printed from the Internet for free. To symbolize the heroine's gifts and strengths—her light—light a white candle and place it in front of the heroine's photograph. Invite the circle to bring items to place on the altar that represents the heroine or the month's affirmation. For example, photographs, items from nature, gemstones, small family heirlooms, books, drawings etc. may be included on the altar. The altar is also the place to keep your Heroines Club Attendance Log and talking stick, if these are elements you wish to include (see below.)

Music

Music affects mood. Instrumental background music played quietly as mothers and daughters enter the space encourages relaxation and tranquility.

Refreshments

From my experience, the girls are always really excited about the snacks! Consider providing drinks and a simple snack, such as fresh fruit, veggie sticks, or cheese and crackers. This could be an area where the responsibility is shared among members, with a different mother/daughter pair providing snacks for the circle each month. Or, you may decide to skip this part altogether! That's fine too.

'Early Bird' Books

On the altar, place the books from the Recommended Resources included in each month's curriculum. Most of these books can be obtained at the local library. Encourage earlier-arriving mothers and daughters to quietly look through the books together while the rest of the circle arrives.

Attendance Log

This is an optional detail, but one that the girls seem to love! Purchase a small, blank journal to use as your Heroines Club Attendance Log, decorating the cover however you wish. Each month, turn to a blank page and write the date, the name of the heroine, and that month's affirmation at the top of the page. Place the log book and a pen on the altar, and as mothers and daughters arrive, invite them to sign in to record their presence in circle that month. This fun little gesture makes the girls feel like they are at an official, secret "club." The Attendance Log also makes a sweet token for posterity.

Talking Stick

The Talking Stick was a method used by Native Americans, to let everyone speak their mind during a council meeting (a type of tribal meeting.) According to the indigenous American's tradition, the stick was imbued with spiritual qualities that called up the spirit of their ancestors to guide them in making good decisions. The stick ensured that all members, who wished to speak, had their ideas heard and that all members of the circle were valued equally.

Consider incorporating a talking stick into your circle to keep the discussion balanced among all participants. During check-ins and discussion, the talking stick is passed around the circle from member to member, allowing only the person holding the stick to speak. Whoever holds the talking stick has within her hands the sacred power of words, and the other circle members direct their full attention to the speaker, remaining silent and practicing sacred witnessing. This enables all those present in circle to have an opportunity to be heard, especially those who may be shy. Of course, circle members are also welcomed to choose to pass the stick and not speak, as silence has a powerful energy as well.

You may wish to make your own talking stick or use some other item, such as a feather, to serve as a talking stick for your circle. Whatever the object, it carries respect for truth-telling and assures the speaker she has the freedom and power to say what is in her heart.

Using the Recommended Resources at Home

Each month's curriculum provides your circle with a list of recommended books and media for mothers and daughters to share at home together. These resources were selected with thorough attention for historical accuracy, age-appropriateness and inspirational value. While there are many resources available in the world, the recommended resources have been carefully vetted for both suitability and quality for your daughter, and are divided into age-appropriate categories. Mothers and daughters are encouraged to get to know the heroine and her story prior to attending that month's circle through the use of these resources, most of which can be found in local libraries and online.

Additionally, curated from the information found in the Recommended Resources, the details of each heroine's life story have been distilled down to the key facts in the Meet the Heroine sections. As you get to know each heroine, it may be helpful to read these condensed storylines with your daughter as well.

Letters to the Mothers

Each month's template begins with a letter written directly to the Heroines Club mothers that offers an introduction to the theme for the month, an exploration of why the topic is so important for our daughters, as well as inspiration and suggestions for bringing the month's topic and affirmation into your home and your relationship with your daughter. Please know, dear woman, these letters were written from my mother-heart to yours.

Each Month's Circle Journey: the Sequence of Events

The sequence of events for each Heroines Club circle should remain consistent throughout the year. Just as when our daughters were little and benefited from being read the same picture books over and over, when we provide a routine and predictable circle structure, daughters will feel safe and secure enough to dive deep within themselves and the circle experience. Below is the recommended sequence of events, time allotments, purpose of each event, and suggestions for successful implementation every step of the way.

Event	Time
Welcoming	Starting 15 minutes before circle begins
Opening Meditation	3 to 5 minutes
Reading of the Commitments	3 to 5 minutes
Check-ins	5 to 10 minutes
Introduction of the Heroine and Reading of the Affirmation	5 to 10 minutes
Discussion Prompts	15 to 20 minutes
Quote Study	10 to 15 minutes
Integrated Activities and Sharing	30 to 45 minutes
Medicine Meditation	3 to 5 minutes
Candlelight Ritual and Song	5 to 8 minutes
Closing Benediction	2 minutes

Welcoming

PURPOSE

Mothers and daughters should be greeted warmly and with enthusiasm, welcoming them into circle and inviting them to make themselves comfortable.

SUGGESTIONS

This time can also be used to briefly touch base and to share any important information with mothers and daughters as they arrive. The facilitator may wish to provide suggestions for what to do before circle begins (find a seat together, place any items you may have brought on the altar, make yourselves comfortable, help yourselves to refreshments, sign in in the log, look through the provided books together, etc.)

Opening Meditation

PURPOSE

The opening meditation officially opens the circle. The purpose is to invite mothers and daughters to relax into the space, begin to synchronize with one another energetically, set their intentions for the circle, and bring their body, mind, and soul fully into the present moment.

SUGGESTIONS

The following meditation can be used verbatim, or feel free to use this as a guide and create your own.

I invite you to find a comfortable, fully-supported resting position and gently close your eyes. You may wish to cuddle up with your mother or with your daughter, or you may wish to hold hands with one another. Begin to notice your breath. Not trying to change anything, just observe the natural rhythm of your breath. Now, breathe deeply and feel the oxygen as it travels into your body, relaxing you even deeper as it fills you with new life. Allow any tension in your body to gently melt away with each deep, cleansing breath.

I invite you to "press pause" on all of the activities and responsibilities occurring outside of this time and space, and land fully present in this moment, this sweet, special time you have carved out and reserved to spend with your beloved daughter, with your beloved mother. What do you hope to receive from our time here together? What do you hope to give? In this next gentle pause, silently set your intentions for our time together. Thank you for being here with us. Your presence in circle is a gift to us all and we are grateful to be sharing the heroines journey with you. Enjoy a few more gentle, cleansing breaths, and when you are ready, open your eyes and make eye contact with your sisters here in circle.

A Reading of the Commitments

PURPOSE

Each circle begins with a reading of the commitments to remind the circle of the agreed upon expectations, as well as to allow each participant an opportunity to use their voice and become comfortable speaking in circle.

SUGGESTIONS

A written copy of the Heroines Club commitments should be passed around the circle, with each participant reading a tenet. Continue passing the copy around until all the commitments have been read. The Heroines Club commitments are:

- ◎ We are all the teachers and we are all the taught.
- ◎ We share from our hearts and speak our truths.
- ◎ What is said in circle stays in circle.
- ◎ We respect the space.
- ◎ We honor our heroines, ourselves and one another, and the mother-daughter relationship.

Check-ins

PURPOSE

Check-ins provide an opportunity for mothers and daughters to experience a sense of belonging to the group and re-establish the connection among members.

SUGGESTIONS

Passing the talking stick around the circle, invite each participant to share how they are feeling, and a response to a check-in prompt.

Use a different check-in prompt each month. Have fun and get creative with this! Potential check-in prompts could be:

- ◎ Something you are particularly proud of about yourself this month.
- ◎ Something you are grateful for right now.
- ◎ Something you and your mother/daughter have in common.
- ◎ Something you really appreciate about your mother/ daughter.
- ◎ Something you are excited about right now.
- ◎ Something you really like about yourself.
- ◎ Something you like about the Heroines Club.

Introduction to the Heroine and Reading of the Affirmation

PURPOSE

To ensure every circle member has the same basic knowledge of the heroine's life story and is reminded of the month's affirmation.

SUGGESTIONS

The facilitator should read the Getting to Know Our Heroine section of that month's curriculum and share the month's affirmation. After reading the information about the heroine and stating the affirmation, open the circle up for general discussion about the heroine and begin passing the talking stick around the circle. This is an open opportunity for mothers and daughters to share whatever is in their hearts regarding the heroine and the month's mantra.

Discussion Prompts

PURPOSE

The discussion prompts provided each month are designed to generate discussion and conscious storytelling about the heroine's life and the month's affirmation, as well as provide mothers and daughters an opportunity to bond together and get to know one another on an even deeper level.

SUGGESTIONS

There are more discussion prompts provided each month than your circle will likely need. Use the questions that most resonate with the developmental level and interest of your circle. Leave space for silence and follow the flow of your circle to know when it is time to move on to the next question. The talking stick can be useful for this element of circle.

Quote Study

PURPOSE

The quotes provided each month were selected for their potency, applicability, universality and dialogue potential for mothers and daughters. The purpose of the Quote Study is to gain familiarity with the wise words spoken by our heroines and to consider how we might apply her wisdom to our own lives.

SUGGESTIONS

Print ready PDFs of each month's full list of quotes can be found at www.TheHeroinesClub.com. Print off or write each of the provided quotes on a separate slip of paper, fold and place them in a small basket or bowl. Pass the basket or bowl around the circle, inviting each participant to choose a quote. Mothers and daughters will then pair up with one another and share their quotes, discussing the meaning and any life applications that can be made. After a few minutes (or when the conversations begin to wane), call the circle back together and allow time for each participant to share their quote and any insights that were gleaned from their private mother-daughter discussions.

Implementing
the Heroines
Club Curriculum

Integrated Activity

The Integrated Activities provided each month allow for a fun, concrete application of that month's affirmation.

Follow the directions provided for each month's Integrated Activity.

Medicine Meditation

The Medicine Meditation allows participants to consider the heroine in her fullness, naming her strengths and gifts, and claiming them also as their own. This element of circle also supports mothers and daughters in connecting with their intuition to apply the month's affirmation to their own lives.

The word medicine comes from the Latin word *medicina*, meaning 'to heal'. When we talk about a heroine's specific medicine, we are referring to her gifts and virtues that offer healing—to both the world collectively and to each of us individually.

Read the Medicine Meditation provided each month. Following the reading, allow time for each participant to speak a word or phrase that they feel best describes the heroine and her medicine, knowing that it is perfectly fine to repeat words that have already been said by another member. Remind the circle that the gifts and virtues that lived within the heroine also live within each of us and that the medicine of our heroines is always available.

Candlelight Ritual and Song

The Candlelight Ritual and Song symbolize our interconnection with the heroine and remind the circle that the qualities that lived within the heroine also live within each one of us.

SUGGESTIONS

Provide a small taper candle for each circle participant. These can be actual candles, or if safety is a concern, battery-operated LED taper candles work well too. If you are using real candles, you will want to provide some sort of drip protector, which can be found at most craft stores.

As a circle, sing the song "Circle of Women" by Nalini Blossom. You may wish to provide written lyrics for the first few gatherings until the circle is familiar with the song. An audio version of the song can be obtained online at https://soundcloud.com/naliniblossom/circle-of-women

And may all mothers know that they are loved,

And may all sisters know that they are strong,

And may all daughters know that they are powerful,

That the circle of women may live on,

That the circle of women may live on . . .

As the circle sings together, mothers and daughters will approach the altar in pairs, lighting their candles from the heroine's candle.

Implementing
the Heroines
Club Curriculum

Continue singing the song until every mother/daughter pair has lit their candles.

Closing

PURPOSE

The circle is closed with a benediction to seal in the magic that was created together and to affirm the gifts received at the Heroines Club.

SUGGESTIONS

With the ritual candles still lit, recite The Heroines Club Benediction together. At the end of the benediction, everyone will blow out their candles and the sacred circle for that month will be closed. You may wish to provide a written copy of the benediction to circle members for the first few gatherings, or until the benediction is memorized.

The Heroines Club Benediction

May we love ourselves.

May we love each other.

May we believe that our dreams can come true.

May we work to make the world a better place.

We are strong.

We are wise.

We are the heroines of our own lives.

Part Two

The Heroines Club: The Complete One-Year Curriculum

AMELIA EARHART

"I Believe in My Dreams"

Dear Mothers,

Our affirmation for this month, inspired by the story of Amelia Earhart, is "I believe in my dreams."

What exactly does this mean and why is a belief in our dreams valuable?

Like seeds planted in the depths of our souls, our dreams are at the center of who we really are. Our mission and our right is to nurture them and to allow them to grow. To follow your dreams takes courage, action, persistence, time and patience, but most of all, you must first *believe* in them. Believing in your dreams means that you trust your aspirations exist for a reason and the reason is your calling. Believing in your dreams means that you hold true that *everything* is possible and you can manifest the life and experiences you desire.

Dreaming is a form of planning; everything we enjoy and appreciate around us—every advancement and contribution to society—developed from the commitment, perseverance and *belief* in its creator's dreams. As wise women, we value dreams as messages from our highest selves and we affirm the messages' worth. Reflect for a moment on a woman you have encountered who believes in

There is a vitality, a life force, an energy, a quickening that is translated through you into action, and because there is only one of you in all of time, this expression is unique. And if you block it, it will never exist through any other medium and it will be lost. You have to keep open and aware directly to the urges that motivate you. Keep the channel open.

Martha Graham

her dreams and actively pursues her desires. You can't keep your admiring eyes off of her! A woman living in harmony with her deepest desires shines brightly like the sun, radiating satisfaction, freedom, happiness and abundance. She lights up everyone around her with her presence. Your dreams, whatever they may be, are not selfish. Believing in our dreams makes space for others to do the same, and uplifts the planet for all.

What if I don't know what my dreams are?

What did you do as a child that made the hours pass like minutes? Therein lies the key to your earthly pursuits.

Carl Jung

A few years ago, I stopped asking children the ever-popular question, "What do you want to be when you grow up?" A much more empowering question is not *what* you want to be, but *who* you want to be. I want to be a woman who is loving, connected, creative, generous, brave, compassionate, kind, courageous, light-hearted, friendly, helpful, smart, passionate, *myself*. This question holds inherent empowerment because it allows our daughters to focus on the present. We should encourage them to cultivate the qualities they wish to embody, knowing that the "what" will unfold naturally over time. In the same way, if you or your daughter are struggling to identify the dreams you have for your life, consider approaching the question from the perspective of *how do I want to feel?*

Discerning how you want to feel is a perfect starting point to begin excavating your dreams. *I want to feel peaceful, safe, grateful, hopeful, loving, comfortable and joyful.* These are your dreams! When do you experience these feelings? As you orient yourself in the direction of your dreams, those moments serve as true North.

Beloved woman, as we get to know Amelia Earhart this month, I invite you to take your dreams down from the shelf where you may have placed them years ago. Dust them off and welcome them back into your heart space and prepare your garden to plant new seeds.

January, the season of resolutions and new beginnings, is the ideal time for this contemplation. *How do you want to feel? What do you want? What are your strongest dreams and deepest desires?*

What if I'm afraid?

To follow your dreams often requires accepting some risks, perhaps the risk of losing money, pride, relationships, time, or in Amelia's case, life itself. We all experience fear in the face of risk. Fear is a natural, healthy emotion and we can allow ourselves to harness its power, and, as Gloria Steinem said, "go forward despite fear." **You don't have to wait for the fear to dissipate before taking action to make your dreams a reality.**

The best way for us to cultivate fearlessness in our daughters and other young women is by example. If they see their mothers and other women in their lives going forward despite fear, they'll know it is possible.

Gloria Steinem

A final thought on dreams

When your daughter shares her dreams with you at home and in circle this month, I encourage you to resist any temptation to reframe her visions in more plausible or lucrative terms. If she dreams of grooming dogs, we needn't rewrite her vision as practicing veterinary medicine. If she dreams of winning the Olympics, we needn't tell her the chances are slim. Dreaming big and in complete alignment with her truest desires is good medicine for our daughters.

What a gift we give our daughters when we encourage them to dream! What a gift it is for our daughters to see their mothers believing in their own dreams! Thank you, Amelia Earhart, for showing us the value of our dreams.

We are in this together.

Love,
Melia

Getting to know our heroine

Amelia Mary Earhart (1897–1937) was a famed aviator, writer, speaker and fashion designer. She was a true pioneer of air travel in the United States, and she is perhaps most well-known for several notable flights, including being the first woman to fly over the Atlantic Ocean and the first person to fly over both the Atlantic and Pacific Oceans.

In the 1920s the airplane was still a new invention. There were no commercial airlines or passenger flights, and few people knew how to fly an airplane. It was even more unusual for a woman to learn to do so. In an era when women were expected to spend their days at home solely committed to domestic pursuits, Amelia rejected society's traditional role for her. She fought hard to overcome the stigma such independence brought upon her. She did not permit anything to prevent her from following her dreams. She was deeply devoted to her family, and Amelia believed that a woman's place was equal to that of a man's not only in aviation, but in all areas of life. She championed women's rights to accomplish their dreams, whatever those dreams may be. Amelia loved life and the living of it, and she recognized the worth of doing things simply for the joy, pleasure and fun of it! Today, this heroine continues to inspire young girls and adult women alike to believe in their dreams and reach for the sky.

Discussion Prompts

1.   Amelia was twenty-three years old when she flew for the first time. She was at a flight show, one of her favorite places to be, and there was an opportunity for her to pay to be a passenger on an airplane ride. In the air, Amelia felt euphoric! She later said that it

was in that moment that she knew her destiny. What is something you love to do that makes you feel euphoric?

2.   All the public attention was hard on Amelia and she often described herself as feeling shy, and yet she gave hundreds of speeches and interviews. Can you relate to this? Do you ever feel shy? What helps you feel more comfortable around others? What helps you feel courageous when speaking in front of others?

3.   At the Women's Air Derby of 1929, many people did not take the women pilots seriously. Will Rogers, a famous social commentator and writer at the time, jokingly called the race the "Powder Puff Derby." Do you feel like gender prejudice still happens today? Have you ever experienced not being taken seriously because you are a woman/girl? How did you handle it?

4.   Amelia came in third place in the 1929 cross country race, the Women's Air Derby. Although she didn't win, she learned a lot and got to know many of the best women pilots in the country. Have you ever had the experience of not winning or succeeding at something, but still getting a lot out of the experience?

5.   Amelia designed a line of women's clothing, specifically created for "active living." She liked clothes that were easy to wash and didn't need special care. If you were a fashion designer, how would you design clothes for girls or women? What is important to you about the clothing you choose to wear?

6.   Mothers, what dreams did you have when you were a little girl? What dreams do you have for yourself today? Daughters, what dreams do you have for your life?

7.   Who do you know among your family, friends, or community that believed in and followed their dreams?

8.   What does this month's affirmation, "I believe in my dreams," mean to you?

Integrated Activity

Create Dream Boards

Inspired by this month's affirmation, mothers and daughters will create dream boards. A dream board is a visual representation of the dreams and goals we want to achieve in our lives, and the things that make us happy. Creating a dream board is a fun and playful way to get in touch with your intuition, to make subconscious connections, and to declare your dreams to the universe. Allowing space to be held to consider your dreams, intentions and desires is the perfect activity to share with your daughter at the beginning of the year.

SUPPLIES

◎ Poster boards cut into the shape of a cloud, representing Amelia's flights in the sky. This month's affirmation can be written on the back of the cloud cut-outs. Provide enough for each mother and each daughter to have their own.

◎ Glue sticks

◎ An abundance of pre-cut photographs from magazines or online images. I have found that the energetic experience of flipping through the pages of a magazine and cutting out pictures is not as helpful as already having images selected to choose from. This also allows mothers to determine the style, range, and tone of the pictures chosen. We want the images to have value for our daughters, representing peace, health, and empowerment. Some examples include pictures of animals, transportation, clouds, flowers, landmarks, objects and powerful words. Pictures on a dream board take on symbolic meaning, for example, a compass could represent travel or direction, and a candle might represent passion or letting one's inner light shine. I recommend having individual plastic bags or large office envelopes containing pictures for each person or each mother-daughter pair to share, rather than one big pile for everyone to choose from. Each individual set should contain a wide assortment of pictures and powerful words from which to choose—much more than will be needed or actually used.

◎ Colorful markers

◎ Timer

INSTRUCTIONS

Take a few deep breaths, calming and opening your heart and mind to the creative journey about to unfold. This is a fun, uplifting activity and there is no wrong way to do it! You may choose to play soft, meditative music in the background, while encouraging mothers and daughters to share the experience by working alongside one another and conversing quietly. You've just discussed what dreams you have for yourselves and this activity will help you take your dreaming a step further. You will be creating dream boards as a visual representation of the things you have discussed in circle and anything else living in your heart. Your boards are cut out in the shape of clouds to remind you of the inspiration you have received from getting to know our heroine, Amelia Earhart. On the back of the board is our affirmation, to remind you that as the heroines of our own lives, we believe in our dreams.

Set the timer for twenty minutes and announce when the last few minutes remain to make any finishing touches. Remind the circle that if they wish to take this activity further, they are invited to continue working on their dream board at home.

STEPS

1.   Look through the provided images and begin making a pile of those that you would like to incorporate into your dream board.

Allow your mind to wander and follow your intuition while making your selections. Choose various pictures that appeal to you. If it catches your eye, there's probably a reason, you may just not know it yet!

2.   Sort through the pictures you have selected and begin to arrange them. You may want to tear parts off, cover-up, or overlap your pictures. Whatever feels positive and creative to you is perfect!

3.   Using the provided glue stick, glue your images onto the board.

4.   If you wish to, you may use the provided markers to decorate your board with doodles or sketches, or write words and affirmations around your images.

After the allotted time is complete, clean the area and gather up the craft supplies. Hold space for each mother and daughter to share her board and give voice to what the images represent for her, while always welcoming anyone to "pass" if they would rather keep their creation private. The dream boards you have just created in circle will remind you of your dreams and keep your heart inspired. Encourage the circle to display them somewhere they will see them often, perhaps in their bedroom or office space.

Medicine Meditation

Set your things to the side, find a comfortable, fully-supported resting position, perhaps take your mother's hand if that would feel good to you, and begin to follow your breath. In your mind's eye, see Amelia. See her flying in an airplane. The cockpit of the plane is wide open. Imagine how the wind feels on her skin. She is wearing aviation goggles, a pilot's cap and a brown leather jacket. Look in her eyes. See her hands on the steering wheel. Is she smiling? Is she contemplative? How does she look and feel to you? What messages is she sending you? What is a word or phrase that describes Amelia, her life and her story, to you? That word or phrase is part of the medicine that Amelia offers us. Take a few more breaths, send your love to Amelia, and when you are ready, open your eyes.

Quote Study

"The most difficult thing is the decision to act, the rest is merely tenacity. The fears are paper tigers. You can do anything you decide to do. You can act to change and control your life; and the procedure, the process is its own reward."

"The more one sees and does and feels, the more one is able to do, and the more genuine may be one's appreciation of fundamental things like home, and love, and understanding companionship."

"Adventure is worthwhile in itself."

"Everyone has oceans to fly, if they have the heart to do it."

"Some of us have great runways already built for us. If you have one, take off. But if you don't have one, realize it is your responsibility to grab a shovel and build one for yourself and for those who will follow after you."

"There is more to life than being a passenger."

Recommended Resources

BOOKS FOR MOTHERS AND DAUGHTERS, AGES 7+

Who Was Amelia Earhart? by Jerome, K.

Amelia Earhart: More Than a Flyer (Ready to Read, Level 3), by Lakin, P.

BOOKS FOR MOTHERS AND DAUGHTERS, AGES 12+

Amelia: A Life of the Aviation Legend, by Goldstein, D.

Sky Pioneer: A Photobiography of Amelia Earhart, by Szabo, C.

FILM FOR MOTHERS AND DAUGHTERS, AGES 12+

Biography—Amelia Earhart (2005)

Amelia (2009)

MUSIC

"Amelia" by Gerry Breslin

"Amelia" by Jim St. James

"Angel Up Above" by Kristina Sablan

WEB

www.ameliaearhart.com/
www.ameliaearhartmuseum.org/

Additional Recommended Resources for Mothers

Big Magic: Creative Living Beyond Fear, by Gilbert, E.

Daring Greatly: How the Courage to Be Vulnerable Transforms the Way We Live, Love, Parent, and Lead, by Brown, B.

A Woman's Worth, by Williamson, M.

Finding Your Own North Star: Claiming the Life You Were Meant to Live, by Beck, M.

FRIDA KAHLO

"I Express My Feelings in Healthy Ways"

Dear Mothers,

Teaching our daughters to feel, tolerate and *express* their feelings is one of the most valuable gifts we can bestow, and this month, inspired by the life and work of our heroine, we will do just that. This higher level of emotional health and intelligence will have a powerful impact on how she takes care of herself, honors herself, and ultimately feels about herself. Like us, our daughters are emotional creatures who experience a beautiful and complex tapestry of feelings. On the journey to young womanhood and beyond, our daughters will experience difficult and painful feelings (as much as we wish we could prevent this from ever happening.) Our goal this month is to explicitly teach our daughters what they can do when those more trying times inevitably come.

Why is this important?

Girls in our culture are socialized to believe that happiness is the singular emotion they may express and still be loved. They are bombarded with the message—from outside and sometimes even inside the home—that achieving the "perfect girl" construct

One of the most effective ways to bolster your daughter's body esteem is to help her develop her emotional intelligence. An awareness of her emotional life can determine how she cares for her body, how she evaluates it, whether she insists that others treat it respectfully, and even whether her body will cooperate as she pursues her dreams. In short, her future success will be determined by whether her mind and body are in conflict or attuned.

Brenda Richardson

properly includes always being cheerful. This limits our daughters, and frankly, it is not safe. Feelings let us know about the state of our needs and are a critical part of the human evolutionary design for survival. When girls repress their "not pretty and not nice" feelings (anger, rage, disappointment, grief, sadness, etc.) and take to heart the old saying, "If you can't say anything nice, don't say anything at all," the price is high. These unpleasant feelings do not disappear. Suppressed emotions, swallowed words and inhibited needs manifest in other ways, such as eating disorders, substance abuse, poor school performance, aggressive behavior, perfectionism, relationship and intimacy problems, depression, anxiety, panic, physical ailments, or simply keeping girls small and attenuated. When feelings are expressed with freedom and confidence, however, they begin to evaporate and heal, and our daughters learn first-hand that experiencing and processing negative feelings is an important part of personal growth.

Things to consider and implement this month

When emotional storms rise, we want our daughters to know empirically that they are still wholly loved and accepted. We also want to ensure that our daughters have tools and strategies in place to comfort and express themselves in healthy ways. They learn this most potently—as with all things—at home.

In your relationship with your daughter this month, I invite you to:

Act as sacred witness to her feelings

"Beloved daughter, I hear you, I see you, and I love you."

What a gift it is when our daughters choose to come to us and share their hearts! Listen to your daughter fully and offer a non-judgmental reflection of her words. Although it is tough to watch our daughters experience hurt, our goal when comforting them should not necessarily be to "rescue" them or make them feel better as quickly as possible. If you are solely focused on helping her feel better—because you are probably feeling pretty upset yourself—you may be missing an opportunity to help her learn and grow from the experience, and you might inadvertently give the impression that it is not okay to be sad or angry. Allow your daughter to share all of her feelings without going into "problem solver" mode or trying to engage in a debate of the facts. We all know how reassuring it feels for our emotional experiences to be acknowledged. Knowing you have been seen and heard makes emotional hardship easier, even if it doesn't solve the situation. Consider the possibility that what she needs most is to release her feelings and be lovingly witnessed.

Remind her that all her feelings are normal

"Beautiful daughter, your feelings are normal"

Big feelings can be scary. Remind your daughter that most people experience weighty, rollercoaster feelings at some point, especially during the rapidly developing ages from eight to fifteen. It can be a great comfort to your daughter to know that whatever she is experiencing, she is not alone.

Don't send her big feelings away

"Powerful daughter, your feelings are not too much for me."

When our daughters experience intense feelings, especially anger, and we send them away to "calm down," they receive the message that their feelings are unacceptable in and of themselves.

Of course, yes, she does need to become calmer before any effective communication can occur, but calming oneself in healthy ways is a skill we learn over time, and usually not on our own.

Welcome her tears

"Wise daughter, let your tears flow without shame."

How often do we tell our daughters not to cry because of our own discomfort with their big emotions? Crying is so good for our daughters (and us!) Crying is a wonderfully effective way to release toxins from our bodies by removing chemicals from the body that build up from stress. Crying is catharsis. We have all experienced how much better we feel after a good cry; the same is true for our daughters.

Let her know it is okay to *not* act happy

"Cherished daughter, it is okay not to smile—you can be authentically you, all the time."

In our culture, girls and women alike are expected to be all smiles and giggles, whether genuine or not. "Give us a smile" is one of the most common catcalls that women receive. Boys, though not necessarily discouraged from smiling, usually aren't cheered on to get happy—or at least look like they are happy. Studies show that this societal pressure is working—women are much more likely to smile than men—and yet, women are twice as likely to suffer from clinical depression. As any woman who has done so can tell you, it hurts the spirit to smile when you are hurting inside. Our daughters feel and develop best when they are free to act in alignment with their authentic inner experiences, regardless of external pressures.

Teach her healthy ways to express her feelings

"Strong daughter, as the heroine of your own life, you express your feelings in healthy ways."

Expressing our feelings will be the focus of our discussion and integrated activity in circle this month. At home, explicitly teach your daughter that expressing her feelings is a healthy part of her self-care. Talking, crying, laughing, singing, stamping, yelling, praying, meditating, making art, making music, dancing, journaling and writing are all wonderful ways to express feelings. What other ways can you think of together?

A final thought on feelings

As mothers, we do not need to completely hide our more painful inner landscapes from our daughters. They do not need a mom who is always happy, and we know such a thing is not realistic anyway. What they need is to witness the healthy, normal ebbs and flows of life, the shifts in mood and energy, and how we ride those out. We give our daughters a gift by allowing them to see us experience, express, and move through all kinds of emotions in healthy ways.

If this is an area of life where you need support—if expressing your feelings in healthy ways is where you struggle—then without any judgment (as we are all still recovering from this long era of patriarchy), I encourage you to seek help. Your healing is her blessing and your healing is worth fighting for.

We are in this together.

Love,
Melia

Getting to Know Our Heroine

Magdalena Carmen Frieda "Frida" Kahlo y Calderón (1907–1954) was a Mexican painter and feminist icon most well known for her intimate and powerful self-portraits. Frida was a strong voice for women at a time when women did not have as many rights as we do now. She was an advocate for indigenous rights, meaning the collective rights of the Mexican people to preserve their unique and traditional culture, and she spoke against commercialization and imperialism. Like her art, Frida's life was complex, fascinating, and inspiring.

Frida had many health problems and injuries that caused her tremendous physical pain. At age six, she contracted polio, which permanently damaged her right leg and confined her to bed for nine months. Then, at eighteen years old, Frida was in a terrible bus accident that broke her spinal cord, collarbone, ribs, pelvic bone, leg, foot, and shoulder, requiring thirty different surgeries and an extensive, life-long recovery. This tragedy changed the course of her life forever.

Prior to the accident, Frida had planned to attend medical school and become a doctor. After the accident, while in constant pain, Frida discovered her love of painting. Because she was so often alone, she had her parents affix a mirror to the ceiling above her bed so she could paint her own portrait and express her innermost feelings. Her works were personal and therapeutic, offering her an outlet to express her intense physical and emotional pain.

Frida wasn't very famous or well-recognized in her lifetime, and there were very few dealers or museums that would host her work—or any woman's work—simply because female artists were considered amateurs in a man's field. Frida never let this stop her! She needed to paint because that was the only positive outlet for her turmoil. How brave she must have been to share her private work, even when she was constantly criticized and misunderstood!

Frida Kahlo continues to be an inspiration for women and girls today, showing the world what a woman is capable of, both physically and emotionally. Frida teaches us that we can, and we must, express all our feelings, even the less pleasant ones.

As we study the life and work of Frida Kahlo this month, I strongly suggest that mothers view her paintings first and choose which to show your daughter. Much of Frida's art may be considered too dark for young children to study.

Discussion Prompts

1.   Frida spent a lot of time alone. Even after the body-cast was removed, on and off for the rest of her life, Frida had to spend months at a time lying in bed. Imagine how bored she must have been for months and months in bed with no television, no iPad, no access to a library . . . Knowing how to be alone and handle boredom is an important skill that will serve you your entire life. How do you experience solitude or boredom?

2.   When Frida was six years old and had contracted polio, she had to spend nine months confined to her bed. During this time, she created an imaginary friend who she would later paint in "The Two Fridas." Did you ever have an imaginary friend? When you were a little girl, what things would you (or do you) like to imagine?

3.   Frida had many pets, including a monkey! If you could have any pet, what would it be?

4.   Pain—both physical and emotional—was a recurring theme in Frida's life. Have you ever experienced great physical or emotional pain? What helped you get through that time?

5.　Do you think a bright side can be found to every tragedy? It was through her tragedy that Frida birthed her passion for painting. Do you think Frida would have become a painter if the near-fatal crash had not occurred? In what ways have hardships led to blessings in your own life?

6.　Frida lived in constant self-expression. This is evident in her art, the way she dressed, and also the way she carried herself. She was known for her exuberant style with her colorful clothes, woven ribbons and flowers in her hair, and lots of jewelry. She liked to wear her monobrow and upper lip hair (normally seen as masculine) proudly even though societal norms expected her to remove it. In what ways do you express yourself and what are you expressing through the clothing choices you make, the ways you style your hair, etc.?

7.　Frida's motto was *"Viva La Vida!"* (Live Life!) What is one of your personal life mottos?

8.　We often only think of common emotions like happy, sad, mad, etc. But the human being experiences a beautiful tapestry of emotions. What are some other feelings and emotions you experience?

9.　What is your favorite feeling to experience? What is your least favorite feeling to experience?

10.　What are some ways that you express your feelings?

11.　What does this month's affirmation, "I express my feelings in healthy ways," mean to you?

Integrated Activities

A Self-Portrait of Feelings and Expressions

This integrated activity allows us the opportunity to creatively explore all the feelings we experience, as well as the many healthy ways we can express our feelings.

SUPPLIES

◎ Template of a head, neck and shoulders drawn with permanent marker on thick, sturdy paper—one for every member of the circle.

◎ Plenty of black Sharpies or other permanent markers

◎ Watercolor paint, water, brushes

INSTRUCTIONS

Our heroine this month teaches us that we can express all of our emotions—even the most uncomfortable ones—in healthy ways. For this integrated activity, inspired by Frida Kahlo, we will create our own self-portraits to represent the healthy expressions of our many different feelings.

STEPS

1. Using the permanent markers provided, write words (or draw symbols and pictures) inside your head and heart space to represent feelings that you experience. Try to think of as many as you can. For example: happy, sad, joyful, brave, cheerful, confused, curious, disappointed, embarrassed, excited, fantastic, friendly, generous, ignored, impatient, important, interested, jealous, lonely, confused, bored, surprised, proud, frustrated, silly, uncomfortable, worried, stubborn, shy, satisfied, safe, relieved, peaceful, overwhelmed, loving, tense, calm.

2.   Using the permanent markers provided, write words (or draw symbols and pictures) to represent healthy things you can do to express your feelings. For example: cry, talk to someone, paint, draw, write a story, write in your journal, yell, dance, sing, punch a pillow, jump up and down, smile and laugh, go for a walk, take a warm bubble bath, pray, meditate, etc.

3.   Using the watercolor paint, brushes and water provided, fill your picture with color. Consider how color might be used to represent different feelings.

After the allotted time is complete, clean the area and gather supplies. Hold space for each mother and daughter to share her self-portrait and give voice to the feelings she experiences and how she expresses them, while always welcoming anyone to "pass" if they would rather keep their creation private. The self-portraits you have just created will remind you of our heroine and affirmation this month.

Laughter Parade

Frida once said, "Nothing is worth more than laughter." Did you know humor and laughter strengthen your immune system, boost your energy, diminish pain, and protect you from the damaging effects of stress? Also, when laughter is shared, it binds people together and increases happiness and intimacy. Give your Heroines Club the medicine of laughter with a "Laughter Parade!" Invite mothers and daughters to pair up, face one another, and have fun experimenting with these different kinds of laughs. Giggles are contagious, and as the old saying goes, "laughter is the best medicine."

1. Laugh like Santa Claus.

2. Laugh like a wicked witch.

3. Laugh like a hyena.

4. Laugh like you are being tickled with a feather.

5. Laugh with your silliest laugh.

6. Laugh with a snort.

7. Laugh with your mouth open wide.

8. Laugh your squeakiest laugh.

9. Laugh like a robot.

10. Laugh like you are on the top of a mountain, hearing your echo.

Medicine Meditation

Set your things to the side, find a comfortable, fully-supported resting position, perhaps take your mother's hand if that would feel good to you, and begin to follow your breath. In your mind's eye, let's travel together to Mexico, to the Blue House that Frida grew up in. Gently open her bedroom door, and see her across the room, propped up in her bed, painting. She sees you enter the room and she is so happy to have a visitor. She invites you over to sit with her in the bed. Enjoy this special time you have with Frida. If you have something you would like to share with her, or ask her, do that now. Listen with your heart for her response. As you look at Frida in this moment, what words come to mind? What is a word, or a phrase, that best describes Frida and her medicine to you? Let's share a few more breaths here with Frida, and when you are ready, offer her your love and gratitude. Tell her, 'thank you for teaching me that I can express my feelings in healthy ways,' and then gently open your eyes and return to our circle.

Quote Study

"My painting carries with it the message of pain."

"I used to think I was the strangest person in the world, but then I thought there are so many people in the world, there must be someone just like me who feels bizarre and flawed in the same ways I do. I would imagine her, and imagine that she must be out there thinking of me, too. Well, I hope that if you are out there, and read this and know that, yes, it's true I'm here, and I'm just as strange as you."

"At the end of the day, we can endure much more than we think we can."

"Nothing is worth more than laughter. It is strength to laugh and to abandon oneself, to be light."

"Nothing is absolute. Everything changes, everything moves, everything revolves, everything flies and goes away."

Recommended Resources

Books for mothers and daughters, ages 7+

Frida, by Winter, J.

Frida Kahlo, by Venezia, M.

Who was Frida Kahlo? by Fabiny, S.

Books for mothers and daughters, ages 12+

The Diary of Frida Kahlo: An Intimate Self-Portrait,
by Fuentes, C.

Frida Kahlo: The Brush of Anguish, by Zamora, M.

Film for mothers and daughters, ages 11+

The Life and Times of Frida Kahlo (2005)

Film for mothers and daughters, ages 16+

Frida (2005)

Web

www.fridakahlo.org
www.museofridakahlo.org.mx

Additional Recommended Resources for Mothers

Building Emotional Intelligence: Practices to Cultivate Inner Resilience in Children, by Lantieri, L.

The Heart of Parenting: Raising Emotionally Intelligent Children,
by Gottman, J.

Opening Up: The Healing Power of Expressing Emotions, by Pennebaker, J.

ISADORA DUNCAN

"My Body is an Instrument"

Dear Mothers,

   This month may be the most revolutionary of all, for we will explicitly teach our daughters to love, accept, honor and celebrate their bodies, *just as they are*. Our bodies are with us from the time we are born until the moment we die, and it is through our bodies that we experience life! What could be more important, or natural, than cultivating a loving relationship with one's body? And yet, so many women and girls are engaged in a raging battle against their own flesh. According to current research:

◎ Nearly half of three- to six-year-old girls worry about becoming fat.

◎ 42% of first to third-grade girls want to be thinner.

◎ 81% of ten-year-old girls are afraid of becoming fat and have admitted to dieting.

◎ 53% of thirteen-year-old girls are unhappy with their bodies.

◎ 78% of seventeen-year-old girls are unhappy with their bodies and 32% of them admit to starving themselves to lose weight.

◎ 65 million American girls and women have reported disordered eating or have an eating disorder.

Complete as the perfect wings of the jay above your head or the pale stars that mark your birth with nothing but pure light. Daughter, I cannot give you anything so complete or perfect or pure. But I can give you something better. Your body . . . and the fierce love of it that no one can take away. And these words will remind you of that love.

Linda Nemec Foster

I see my body as an instrument, rather than an ornament.

Alanis Morissette

This long era of patriarchy has really damaged the relationship women and girls have with their bodies. Girls are taught by the mainstream media, fashion and retail industries, friends and sometimes family, and even the health and fitness industries that *the way they look is of maximum importance and their physical appearance is tantamount to their value in society*. Because of this lie, many young girls suffer from devastating issues around body image. In my work with women, I have yet to meet a woman who has not at some time struggled with loving and accepting her body, myself very much included. The narrow standard of what is desirable, or even *acceptable*, for the female body is a poison that is affecting female progress in every way, from greater instances of depression, anxiety, disordered eating, to wasted time, energy, and resources. Habitual body monitoring, which is encouraged by our sexually objectifying culture, reduces the overall quality of our lives and crowds out our ability to develop a variety of deeper and more important values.

Even as women have made enormous progress in education, politics, and industry, women and girls still struggle with loving themselves when they look in the mirror. If there is to be a serious advance in the status of Western women, we need a widespread rebellion of women who refuse to play along with society's rigid body expectations any longer, and who are determined to raise their daughters with a positive and healthy body image. This, dear mothers, is the final frontier of the women's movement, and we are joining arms in solidarity to protect our daughters and to heal ourselves.

The importance of cultivating a positive body image in our girls cannot be understated; how our daughters think about and respect their physical selves will impact everything they do and every decision they make. As mothers, we can help create the recording that our daughters play in their heads throughout the day when they look in the mirror, walk the halls of their schools, and someday go out on dates. May they always hear us, loud and clear, telling them that their amazing bodies are perfect, *just the way they are,* and may they believe us.

Together this month, inspired by our heroine, we will build confidence and appreciation for the things our bodies can *do,* rather than just how they look. We will encourage our daughters to think of their bodies as the sacred instruments they use to express themselves and experience life, rather than mere ornaments that exist for the viewing and enjoyment of others. In this way, we will explore with our daughters the importance of caring for their body-instrument by developing a loving relationship with their bodies.

A final note to mothers: if body image or caring for your body is an area where you struggle, with all compassion and understanding, I encourage you to seek out support for your healing. Your healing is her blessing, and your healing is worth fighting for.

We are in this together.

Love,
Melia

Getting to Know Our Heroine

Angela Isadora Duncan (1877–1927), often referred to as the "Mother of Modern Dance," was a trailblazing dancer and instructor whose emphasis on freer forms of movement was a precursor to modern dance techniques. She was among the first to raise interpretive dance to the status of creative art.

From an early age, Isadora was passionate about dancing. At only six years old, Isadora began teaching movement to other little children in her San Francisco, California neighborhood. With her accomplished pianist mother as accompanist and her sister as partner, these lessons became a successful endeavor, earning income for her family. At the time, the only socially acceptable forms of dance available to women were ballet, burlesque and theatrical dance. Rather than just entertain an audience by executing the given choreography, Isadora wanted the freedom to move in ways that were natural, expressive and spontaneous. At the age of twenty-one, Isadora moved to Europe to continue developing her art.

Isadora's methods and ideas about dance were revolutionary, and like many of our heroines, she was often criticized by others for not following the status quo in her field. Inspired by Greek art, the paintings of Sandro Botticelli, Walt Whitman's poems, the instinctual movements of children and animals, and great classical music, Isadora stripped dance of all ornamentation and took movement back to the basics. She discarded conventional dance costumes in favor of Greek tunics, bare feet and loose hair, to allow the greatest possible freedom of movement. Isadora danced with movements originating from her solar plexus, the area located beneath the sternum, where she believed the soul resides. Her methods were unprecedented and revolutionary, both for the art world and the socio-political sphere.

Although Isadora struggled financially, she rejected lucrative invitations to perform in the popular Vaudeville circuit variety shows. Risqué and rowdy in nature, the Vaudeville movement relegated women to the role of ornaments and sexual entertainment for male enjoyment and this went against everything Isadora believed to be true about dance as a form of personal expression. Isadora strove to change the view of women's roles and the female body from sexual to artistic, and in doing so, she changed dance from mere entertainment to higher art.

Isadora's dream was to influence young children to express themselves and cultivate healthy relationships with their bodies through dance. Subsidized by her dance tours, Isadora opened many free-of-charge dance schools across Europe and Russia. The young girls were not only educated by these schools, but many of the previously homeless students were homed, and given a standard scholarly education in addition to their dance curriculum.

Throughout her life, Isadora remained a gifted performer and committed dance teacher, showing the world that the female body was not an ornament of sexuality, but an instrument for self-expression. Isadora's legacy of body empowerment continues to inspire women and girls today.

Discussion Prompts

1.   Do you enjoy dancing? How does it make your body feel to dance? What feelings or emotions do you express through dancing?

2.   In the early 1900s, most women were still wearing restrictive corsets under their dresses to trap and train the torso into a desired shape for "beauty" purposes. What do you think of corsets? Are there any versions of "corsets" that still exist for women today?

3.   Do you think Isadora experienced peer pressure? How would her legacy have differed if she had let peer pressure impact her actions or if she had she succumbed to what society and others were doing around her?

4.   How have ideas about body image in our society changed over time? What do you think have caused these changes? Do you think they will shift again in the future?

5.   How are ideas about body image different in other parts of the world? What do you think accounts for this?

6.   Do you have friends who talk about their weight and dieting?

How does it make you feel? How do you handle those conversations?

7.   What is something your body can *do* that you are really proud of?

8.   What are some ways that you care for your body? How does your body let you know what it wants and needs?

9.   What are some activities you enjoy that make you feel good in your body?

10.   Who or what supports you in experiencing your body in a positive way?

11.   What does this month's affirmation, "My Body is an Instrument," mean to you?

Integrated Activities

"The Skin I'm In" Meditation

The human body is a miracle! When we place our value and focus on how our bodies look on the outside, we often forget all of the incredible things our bodies do for us, day in and day out, on the inside. Appreciating your body for all the complex internal magic it performs is a great way to re-shape the dialogue you have with yourself about your body.

Read the following meditation aloud to your circle, and together, take a journey inward to converse with the amazing instrument of your body.

Take a deep breath in and as you exhale, imagine that your consciousness is so light that it can float up and out of your physical body. In your mind's eye, allow yourself to gently rise up above your body, and see yourself, just as you are, here in our circle.

With loving compassion and unconditional acceptance, observe your physical body—your instrument—from this vantage point. Take a moment now to see yourself as you would gaze upon a beloved friend, or as a mother would her daughter. Feel in your heart the unconditional love and gratitude for all that your body does for you.

Notice the largest organ of your body—your skin. Your skin creates the boundary between yourself and the rest of the world. It protects and contains you. Take a moment now to tune in to your skin. Ask your skin what she wants and needs, and listen to her reply. Thank your skin for her devotion to you.

I invite you now to shift your consciousness to your muscles and bones and joints—the parts that move you. Your body was built to move! Tune in with your bones and muscles now, and ask your musculoskeletal system what she wants and needs. What movement does your body crave? What physical practice would nourish and strengthen you? Thank your muscles and bones for their devotion to you.

And now shift your awareness to your cardiovascular and respiratory systems—your heart, lungs and blood. The home of your breath and seat of your emotional body, your lungs and heart work without rest to fuel your body with oxygen and nourishment for all of the work and play and passion that you choose. Ready in an instant, your cardiovascular and respiratory systems are on stand-by 24/7 to serve you. I invite you now to tune in with your heart, and lungs, and blood and ask them what they want and need. Feel the rhythm and the pulse of your body, and thank your heart and blood and lungs for their devotion to you.

I invite you now to shift your awareness to your digestive system—your stomach and intestines. Tasked with sorting through all that you eat and drink, and separating the nourishing from the unusable, your digestive system keeps your cells fueled and functional. Take a moment now to tune in with your digestive system. Gently, kindly, ask your digestive system what would nurture and nourish her, and listen for the answer. Thank your digestive system for its devotion to you.

And lastly, I invite you to shift your awareness to your nervous system—your brain and nerves. The control center of your physical body, your nervous system makes the commands and sends them out while simultaneously integrating the incoming data stream from all of your five senses and also thinking thoughts and dreaming dreams and analyzing information without you being consciously aware of it all happening! That is quite a feat! Breathing in now with a sense of well-being and calm, I invite you to tune in with your nervous system and ask her what she most needs and wants; what would calm and nourish her? Listen for the answer. Thank your nervous system for her devotion to you.

With a deep breath in, I invite you now to gently rejoin your physical self, reintegrate your consciousness and your body. Feel the weight of your hands and legs being supported by the floor. Feel the rhythm of your heart, and the cycling of your breath. When you are ready, open your eyes.

Following the meditation, hold space for sharing and reflection among circle participants.

◎ What was your experience with this meditation?

◎ What wants and needs did your various body systems communicate?

◎ How did it feel to offer gratitude to your body?

◎ How might you incorporate this kind of conversation with your body on a daily basis?

Body Praise Circle

Positive body talk does not happen naturally in our culture. Women often bond over body bashing, and our daughters hear us. Let us hold some space for body love and appreciation! The Body Praise Circle activity offers our daughters an opportunity to witness women loving and appreciating their bodies, and to hear the many diverse and important ways we use our bodies as instruments.

As a child, I never heard one woman say to me, 'I love my body.' Not my mother, my elder sister, my best friend. No one woman has ever said, 'I am so proud of my body.' So I make sure to say it (to my daughter) because a positive physical outlook has to start at an early age.

Kate Winslet

INSTRUCTIONS

1.   Sitting in circle, the facilitator begins by saying, "I love my legs because they help me _____." She then asks the person beside her, "Why do you love your legs?" That person will respond in turn with "I love my legs because they help me_____," and then ask the person beside her "Why do you love your legs?" This continues until everyone in the circle has had a chance to respond.

2.   Carry on with this pattern, inserting various parts of the body, such as arms, feet, hands, legs, mouth, eyes, ears, breasts, toes, belly, fingers, etc . . .

3.   The final round of the Body Praise Circle will be dedicated to offering appreciation to our bodies as a whole. The facilitator will begin with "I love my body because ____," and then ask the person beside her, "Why do you love your body?" This will continue until everyone in the circle has had a chance to respond.

At the end of the activity, hold space for sharing and reflection among circle participants:

◎   What was your experience with this activity?

◎   Was it hard for you to think of why you loved various parts of your body?

◎   What was your comfort level when expressing praise for your body?

◎ How did it feel to hear other women and girls expressing love for their bodies?

◎ How might you incorporate this kind of body talk into your daily life?

Body-Love Dancing

SUPPLIES

◎ Scarves or ribbons

◎ Classical music, such as Vivaldi's *The Four Seasons*

INSTRUCTIONS

Invite circle participants to remove their shoes and socks and dance together barefoot the way Isadora did! Play classical music, like that to which Isadora danced, and encourage the mothers and daughters to move their bodies in any way that feels good and nourishing. Providing ribbons or scarves is a great way to encourage full-body movement and fun.

Medicine Meditation

Set your things to the side, find a comfortable, fully-supported resting position, perhaps take your mother's hand if that would feel good to you, and begin to follow your breath. In your mind's eye, let's travel together to one of Isadora's dance schools, where she is teaching young students. In the large multi-mirrored room, we see Isadora sitting on the floor with her students gathered around her. She is speaking to them. Isadora notices you at the door, and with a friendly smile, she invites you in to join the other young girls. As you join the group on the floor, Isadora resumes speaking. What is she telling you and the other girls about movement? What is she telling you about your body? Do you have a question for Isadora? If you do, feel free to raise your hand and ask her. She wants to share her knowledge and passion with you. What message does Isadora have for you? Receive her words and thank her for teaching you that your body is a beloved instrument for self-expression and experiencing life. Thank her for teaching you that your body is perfect just the way it is. As you look at Isadora here in this moment, what words come to mind? What words or phrases describe the medicine of Isadora Duncan to you? When you are ready, send her your love and gratitude, and gently open your eyes and return to our circle.

Quote Study

"You were once wild here. Don't let them tame you!"

"My motto: sans limites."

"The dancer's body is simply luminous manifestation of the soul."

"People don't live nowadays: they get about ten percent out of life."

"The finest inheritance you can give to a child is to allow it to make its own way, completely on its own feet."

"If I could tell you what it meant, there would be no point in dancing it."

"I do not teach children; I give them joy."

"Let us first teach little children to breathe, to vibrate, to feel, and to become one with the general harmony and movement of nature. Let us first produce a beautiful human being, a dancing child."

"My art is just an effort to express the truth of my Being in gesture and movement. It has taken me long years to find even one absolutely true movement."

Recommended Resources

Books for Mothers and Daughters, ages 7+

Isadora Dances, by Isadora, R.

Isadora Duncan, by Keating, S.

Books for Mothers and Daughters, ages 12+

Isadora Duncan: A Graphic Biography, by Jones, S.

Barefoot Dancer: The Story of Isadora Duncan, by O'Connor, B.

Film

Isadora Duncan: Movement from the Soul (1989)

Web

http://www.isadoraduncan.org/

http://www.idii.org/

Additional Recommended Resources for Mothers

The Body Project: An Intimate History of American Girls,
by Brumberg, J.

101 Ways to Help Your Daughter Love Her Body,
by Richardson, B. and Rehr, E.

You Have to Say I'm Pretty, You're My Mother: How to Help Your Daughter Learn to Love Her Body and Herself,
by Pierson, S. and Cohen, P.

You'd Be So Pretty If … Teaching Our Daughters to Love Their Bodies — Even When We Don't Love Our Own, by Chadwick, D.

JACKIE JOYNER-KERSEE

"I Challenge Gender Stereotypes and Discrimination"

Dear Mothers,

It is difficult for many of us, and certainly for our daughters, to fully understand how far we have come in regard to women's rights. Women around the world have fought for centuries, protesting for the rights of women to bodily integrity and autonomy, to vote, to hold public office, to sexual and reproductive rights, to equal pay, to own property, to education, to serve in the military, to enter into legal contracts, to marital rights, and to parental rights. All the changes for women that have been achieved throughout history did not just happen spontaneously; women very deliberately *made* these changes happen.

Let's take a walk together down Women's History lane, and give thanks for all the work and progress that has been accomplished on our behalf. As suffragette Abby Foster once said, "Bloody feet, sisters, have worn smooth the path by which we have come up hither."

Men, their rights and nothing more; women, their rights and nothing less.

Susan B. Anthony

1848: The first women's rights convention is held in Seneca Falls, New York.

1869: Susan B. Anthony and Elizabeth Cady Stanton form the National Women's Suffrage Association.

1872: Susan B. Anthony casts a ballot in the presidential election, though women were prohibited from doing so. Two weeks later, she was arrested, tried, and found guilty of illegal voting.

1893: New Zealand becomes the first self-governing country to grant all women over the age of twenty-one the right to vote in Parliamentary elections.

1895: Women in South Australia achieve the right to vote.

1913: Emily Wilding Davison throws herself under the King's horse to bring the world's attention to the cause of Women's Suffrage. Norwegian women gain the right to vote.

1916: Margaret Sanger opens the first U.S. birth control clinic in Brooklyn, New York. She is arrested ten days later.

1918: Women in the UK and Ireland over the age of thirty are granted the right to vote. Ten years later, the right is extended to women ages twenty-one and older.

1920: The 19th Amendment to the U.S. Constitution is signed into law, granting women the right to vote.

1928: Women compete for the first time in Olympic field events.

1934: Women in Brazil and Thailand gain the right to vote.

1946: Women in the Philippines gain the right to vote.

1949: Women gain the right to vote in Israel and South Korea.

1954: Columbian women are granted the right to vote.

1960: The U.S. Federal Drug Administration approves birth control pills.

1961: The President's Commission on the Status of Women is established in the U.S. documenting substantial discrimination against women in the work place and making specific recommendations for improvement.

1963: Betty Friedan publishes her highly influential book, *The Feminine Mystique*, galvanizing the modern women's rights movement. U.S. Congress passes the Equal Pay Act, making it illegal for employers to pay a woman less than a man would receive for the same job.

Iranian women gain the right to vote.

1969: California becomes the first U.S. state to adopt a "no fault" divorce law with equal distribution of common property.

1971: *Ms. Magazine* is first published and Gloria Steinem is launched as an icon of the modern feminist movement.

Women in Switzerland gain the right to vote.

1972: Title IX of the Education Amendment bans sex discrimination in any federally-funded educational program or activity in the U.S. The enrollment of women in athletic programs increases dramatically.

1974: Argentina has the first female president.

1977: Nigerian women gain the right to vote.

1978: For the first time in history, more women than men enter college. The Pregnancy Discrimination Act bans employment discrimination against pregnant women.

1981: The first "National Women's History Week" is proclaimed by the U.S. president. Sandra Day O'Connor becomes the first woman appointed to the U.S. Supreme Court.

1987: In America, "National Women's History Week" becomes "Women's History *Month*."

1986: The U.S. Supreme Court declares that sexual harassment is a form of illegal job discrimination.

1993: "Take Our Daughters to Work Day" debuts.

2013: The ban on women serving in combat roles is lifted in the U.S.

So, it's all good now, right? The war for equal rights for women is over? No, sadly, it is not; the battle for equality continues.

Although profound changes have been made for women, it is folly to believe that discrimination against women is already in our collective past. Despite women's advancements, substantial inequalities persist. Women and girls continue to face gender discrimination in industry, in legal proceedings, in the home, in the medical field, in media and marketing tactics, in the education system, and in the church. Despite making up 50.8% of the world's population, women today:

◎ Earn only 10% of the world's income and own only 1% of the world's property.

◎ Make up just 4.6% of the CEOs of the 500 largest corporations in the U.S.

◎ Continue to experience a gender wage gap of 16% in the U.S. even after over fifty years of legislation.

◎ Hold only 18.3% of U.S. congressional seats, and only 23% of statewide elective offices.

◎ Are offered no paid maternity leave policy mandated by law in the U.S.

◎ Spend nearly twice as much time on housework as compared to men, regardless of career status.

◎ Have a statistically significant disadvantage when applying for highly selective universities, despite the fact that women generally outperform men in high school.

◎ Make up only 1/3 of physicians today and earn 37% less than their male counterparts.

◎ Are mostly excluded from leadership roles in most religions.

◎ Comprise less than a quarter of film protagonists, and only 29% of speaking characters in top Hollywood movies.

◎ Hold less than 25% of science, technology, engineering, and math jobs.

Our daughters absorb insidious messages of gender stereotypes, consciously and subconsciously, every day.

During the last week of public school in 2013, my son's first grade class was celebrating the end of the year with different themed events all week—wear your pajamas to school on Monday; on Tuesday, bring a board game from home; on Wednesday, bring a towel for water play, and then on Thursday, this:

> *"Today will be a 'Girls Day In / Boys Day Out.' Girls may bring a doll or a stuffed animal and boys may bring a ball or sports equipment. Students will enjoy creative play and a sports game with their first grade friends."*

I was shocked! Upon receiving this note in my son's backpack, I wrote to his teacher and the school's principal, and firmly brought to their attention that this kind of activity was sending a terrible message to children. Thankfully, the plan for the day was changed, but the damage had been done: our children had heard from adults they loved and respected that their interests should be determined based on their gender.

In 2014, I took my two younger children to the doctor's office for a check-up. As we were leaving, a helpful and kind nurse offered my children a prize from the "treasure box." My daughter spent quite a while digging through the box, finally making her choice: a temporary-tattoo depicting a sports car. The nurse quickly reached in the box and thrust forward a temporary-tattoo featuring a smiling, decorated hippopotamus, and said, "Why don't you give that one to your brother. Here's one that's more for a girl." Again, I was stunned at the blatant stereotyping and told the nurse, "We believe car tattoos are for everyone," but once again, the damage had been done: my beloved daughter had received the message from a person in authority that it is wrong to step outside of one's gender box.

These are just two of my personal stories; I'm sure you have your own stories of stereotyping and discrimination to add to the pyre. Some may say that these stories are "not that big of a deal." Some may say that these stories are innocent, harmless mistakes born from ignorance. When our daughters are taught limits on "girl" choices, it puts limits on who they can *be*. What at seven years old is cars and hippos, or balls and dolls, becomes science and home-economics at fifteen years old, and seventy-seven cents to the dollar at thirty years old.

Our society considers gender to be an important determinant of abilities and interests. From infancy, our culture tries to dictate what it means to be a girl or a boy. Children who do not adopt the traditional gender roles are often targeted for harassment or bullying. This is wrong and it *is* a "big deal." Gender stereotypes play a significant role in defining our daughters' lives and their aspirations for the future.

Raising an empowered daughter in this culture of discrimination is exacting and challenging, but it is possible. Teaching our daughters to first become aware of, and then to deconstruct and challenge gender stereotypes helps them make decisions on how to look, act, and live based on their *individual thoughts and feelings*, rather than on societal expectations. Our goal this month is to help our daughters develop their own critical intelligence with regard to culturally inherited stereotypes, to let them know that they have our full support in challenging gender stereotypes and discrimination, and perhaps the most important of all: to let our daughters know they have both our permission and our blessing to be **exactly who they are.**

It is best to encourage girls to grow up informed of the common forms of discrimination that they are likely to face, and to develop strategies from a young age to take responsibility and stand strong in the face of adversity. This month, inspired by our heroine, we will do just that.

We are in this together.

Love,
Melia

Getting To Know Our Heroine

Jacqueline "Jackie" Joyner-Kersee (born March 3, 1962) overcame discrimination, poverty and disease to become one of the greatest athletes of all time.

Jackie grew up in East St. Louis, Illinois, a poverty-stricken city on the Mississippi River. Her parents were teens when they married. Her mother was only fourteen years old when she gave birth to Jackie's older brother and sixteen years old when she gave birth to Jackie. Her parents worked hard, and they knew real desperation and hardship. The family often had to sleep in the kitchen because the stove was the only source of heat in the house. Jackie's older brother, Al, himself an Olympic gold medalist, told *Sports Illustrated*: "I remember Jackie and me crying together in the back room in that house, swearing that someday we were going to make it. Make it out. Make things different." Having endured the hardships of teen motherhood and wanting a better life for her children, Jackie's mother had very strict rules for her children and placed a high value on education.

Jackie was a natural athlete and she always enjoyed sports. At that time, however, girls were not allowed to play sports at school other than cheerleading. Jackie was ten years old when Title IX was passed in 1972, which granted girls the right to play sports at school. Even with that legislation in place, girls continued to experience tremendous discrimination in athletics, and there was little value placed on women's sports. In fact, many people viewed women's competitive sports as *unfeminine*. Jackie challenged gender stereotypes and pursued her passion for sports in full force.

Jackie received widespread honors in high school in various sports, including track, basketball and volleyball. She was also an excellent student, finishing in the top 10% of her graduating class.

With the help of her loving family and the positive influence of the volunteers at the local youth center, Jackie stayed away from drugs, alcohol, violence and teen pregnancy—not an easy thing to do in East St. Louis at that time. Jackie graduated high school and attended the University of California, Los Angeles on a full basketball scholarship. While a top student-athlete at UCLA, Jackie was diagnosed with asthma, a respiratory condition that makes it hard to breath at times. She hid her diagnosis from her coaches, fearing it would end her athletic career. Eventually, Jackie realized that she needed to be honest with her coaches and take her medicine regularly if she wanted to succeed. In 1985, Jackie graduated from UCLA with a major in history and began intensive training for the Olympics.

Jackie worked hard, trained hard, and persevered to make her dreams come true. At the end of her Olympic career, Jackie had won six medals, including three gold medals. Her gold medal-winning score from the 1988 heptathlon, a grueling track-and-field event, still stands as the world record. In 2000, she was voted the Greatest Female Athlete of the 20th century by *Sports Illustrated*.

Following her retirement in 2001, Jackie returned to her impoverished hometown, committed to give back to the community that had shaped her character. She founded the Jackie Joyner-Kersee Youth Center Foundation, which provides educational and recreational programs for underprivileged youth. She is also a popular motivational speaker and role model for asthma sufferers. Jackie Joyner-Kersee continues to inspire women and girls today to challenge gender stereotypes and overcome gender discrimination.

Discussion Prompts

1. According to Joyner family lore, Jackie was named by her paternal grandmother, who chose the name "Jacqueline" after the wife of then U.S. President, John F. Kennedy. On the back of a baby picture of Jackie, her grandmother wrote, "She will someday be the first lady of something!" Jackie did become the first lady of something: track and field! Are you named after anyone? What is the story of how you got your name?

2. When Jackie entered her first competitive track meet, she finished dead last. After this defeat, she began training harder and was soon winning her meets. Jackie exhibited determination by refusing to quit, even when she didn't first succeed. When have you exhibited determination and perseverance in your own life?

3. When Jackie was defeated in the long jump by her friend,

Heike Drechsler of Germany, she congratulated her with a hug and kind words. Do you imagine it was hard for Jackie to display such good sportsmanship? Why is it important to treat your opponents with respect and kindness, whether you win or lose?

4.   Gender discrimination has existed since the beginning of athletic competitions. The modern Olympics, one of the most popular sporting events in the world, didn't allow women to compete in competitions when they first began in Greece in the late 19th century. It was not until 2012 that all participating Olympic teams had female athletes. In what ways have you witnessed or experienced gender discrimination in sports? How did it make you feel? How did you handle it?

5.   Do you see any ways in which girls are shamed today when they do not act "feminine" enough?

6.   Have you ever faced gender stereotypes when you were pursuing an interest that others did not support? What did you do?

7.   Have you or someone you know ever stood up for a person who challenged gender stereotypes?

8.   What should you do if someone says you can't play in their game because you are a girl? ("You can't say girls can't play!") Or someone says you can't do something because you are a girl? ("Not true! Gender doesn't limit you!") Or someone says that your clothes, hair, or actions are wrong because of your gender? ("There's no such thing as boys' ____ or girls' ____!")

9.   Imagine you woke up one morning and you found out that for some mysterious reason you had been transformed into a boy. Would you want to try something new that perhaps you felt you couldn't do while you were a girl? What would it be?

10.   What do you like about being a girl? What don't you like about being a girl?

11. What messages would you give to a younger girl about being female today?

12. What does this month's affirmation, "I Challenge Gender Stereotypes and Discrimination," mean to you?

Integrated Activities

See It To Be It!

Together as a circle, go see a women's high school, college, amateur or professional sporting event! Consider going to an event that is not culturally characterized as feminine (i.e. an event other than gymnastics, figure skating, cheerleading, etc.) Cheer on these amazing athletes!

Thinking Outside the (Gender) Box

A first step to overcoming stereotyped thinking is to be aware of what stereotypes people hold.

SUPPLIES

◎ Large dry-erase board

◎ Marker

◎ Eraser

INSTRUCTIONS

1. Define gender (whether you are a boy or a girl) and stereotype (the expectation that all members of a group are similar with no

individual differences) for the circle. Give examples of stereotypes (for example, "all blondes are dumb") and explain that for this activity, you will be exploring stereotypes based on gender.

2.   On the dry-erase board, draw two large boxes, one representing "girl" stereotypes and one representing "boy" stereotypes.

3.   Beginning with the "girl" box, ask the circle the following questions and write their words or phrases in the box.

How are girls "supposed" to behave?

What are girls "supposed" to like and dislike?

How are girls "supposed" to look/think/feel?

What are girls "supposed" to be good at?

(Examples are: loves to shop, likes to draw and paint, wears makeup, has long hair, loves babies, emotional, likes to dance, pretty, likes dolls, wears dresses and skirts, likes the color pink, good at reading, quiet, helpless, most of friends are girls, etc.)

4.   Moving to the "boy" box, ask the circle the following questions and write their words or phrases in the box.

How are boys "supposed" to behave?

What are boys "supposed" to like and dislike?

How are boys "supposed" to look/think/feel?

What are boys "supposed" to be good at?

(Examples are: plays video games, enjoys outdoor activities, good at math and science, likes sports, never cries, likes cars, strong, athletic, likes to get dirty, loud, takes out the garbage, wears jeans, fixes things, most friends are boys, etc.)

5.   Spend a moment looking at the two boxes. Remind the circle that these boxes include things that girls and boys are "supposed" to do or be like, not what they might actually be like. Ask the circle:

When you look at these lists, how do you feel?

Are there any attributes that apply to everyone who is a girl or boy? (No.)

Is there anything in the girl box that boys are not able to do? (No.)

Is there anything in the boy box that girls are not able to do? (No.)

What might happen if someone steps outside of her/his box or doesn't fit in her/his box?

Remind the circle that while some people fit a gender stereotype more than others, almost everyone sometimes feels "outside the box," and that while most children's gender identity (the sense of being a girl or a boy) aligns with their biological sex, for some children, gender identity is not so clear, and the sense of being "other," "both," or "neither" best describes their reality—and that too is perfectly okay.

6.   To avoid reinforcing the stereotypes (rather than subverting them), it is necessary to end with a discussion. Erase the boxes, leaving only the words and phrases, to demonstrate equality. Explain that each person has individual desires, thoughts and feelings, regardless of their gender, and that we have a right to be exactly who we are. We don't have to accept the limits of stereotypes; we have the power to decide what makes sense for us!

Medicine Meditation

Set your things to the side, find a comfortable, fully-supported resting position, perhaps take your mother's hand if that would feel good to you, and begin to follow your breath. In your mind's eye, travel with me to the running track where Jackie is practicing in East St. Louis, Illinois. The sun is shining and the temperature feels just right on your skin. You arrive just as Jackie is finishing her last lap for today's training session. She is running at full speed, her strong legs plowing the ground beneath her, her strong arms pumping the air around her, and her expression determined as she focuses on the finish line. Wow! Take in the full beauty and strength of Jackie in this moment.

As you look at Jackie, think of a word or phrase that describes her life and her story to you. Jackie finishes her last lap. She bends over, places her hands on her knees, and breathes heavily. You now approach Jackie and offer her a drink of water, which she gratefully accepts with a smile. Jackie invites you to sit down and join her for a conversation. What would you like to ask Jackie? You may ask her anything. What does Jackie tell you about her life? What advice does she offer you about your life? What words of wisdom does Jackie have just for you? Thank Jackie for showing the world just how strong and powerful women can be. Thank her for challenging gender stereotypes and discrimination, and for encouraging you to do the same. Take a few more breaths here with Jackie, send her your love, and when you are ready, open your eyes.

Quote Study

"I don't think being an athlete is unfeminine. I think of it as a kind of grace."

"There are many women who came before me who didn't really have the same opportunities that I have had. That's why I always wanted to be a great ambassador—not only to today's generation—but for the women who really didn't have a voice, but who paved the way for me."

"Your environment doesn't define you. I don't have a lot of money, but I can help train people and I can talk to people. We can all be mentors to the next generation."

"When I was in elementary school, we weren't allowed to do sports other than cheerleading. By junior high, they let us play, but we had to come back after 6:30pm to practice because there was only one gymnasium and the boys used it first."

Recommended Resources

Books for Mothers and Daughters, ages 7+

Jackie Joyner-Kersee: Superwoman, by Goldstein, M.

Jackie Joyner-Kersee, by Cohen, N.

Books for Mothers and Daughters, ages 12+

A Kind of Grace: An Autobiography of the World's Greatest Female Athlete, by Jackie Joyner-Kersee

A Woman's Place is Everywhere, by Jackie Joyner-Kersee

Jackie Joyner-Kersee: Champion Athlete, by Harrington, G.

Film for Mothers and Daughters, ages 12+

Miss Representation (2011)

Suffragette (2015)

Web

http://jackiejoynerkersee.com/

http://jjkfoundation.org/

Additional Recommended Resources for Mothers

Redefining Girly: How Parents Can Fight the Stereotyping and Sexualizing of Girlhood, from Birth to Tween, by Wardy, M.

Cinderella Ate My Daughter, by Orenstein, P.

Pink Brain, Blue Brain, by Eliot, L.

ANNE FRANK

"I Am Resilient in the Face of Adversity"

Dear Mothers,

This month, we are going to introduce our daughters to an inspiring young heroine, the beloved Anne Frank. For *some* of our daughters, this will also mean learning for the first time about the Holocaust. Your intuition may guide you to know that the details of the Holocaust are not appropriate for your daughter's age and/ or emotional developmental level at this time. I encourage you to practice sovereignty in introducing this material, and to follow your instincts and your daughter's lead. The recommended resources listed at the end of this chapter are a safe, age-appropriate place to start. In my experience, I have found that in working with younger girls (age 8–9), the details of the Holocaust and the concept of genocide are indeed unnecessary in introducing the story of Anne Frank; it is enough to simply say she was a girl who lived through a massive war which required her family to live in hiding. For girls ten and older, however, the topic of genocide may be introduced and discussed if the girls demonstrate appropriate emotional readiness. This month, hand in hand with our daughters, we will explore the life of our heroine and discuss the concept of resilience.

Above all, be the heroine of your life, not the victim.

Nora Ephron

Resilience

How did Anne Frank, in the midst of living in extreme fear and hiding, pen statements such as *"I must uphold my ideals, for perhaps the time will come when I shall be able to carry them out"*? How do humans recover from trauma? The answer lies in the concept of *resilience*.

The word 'resilience' comes from the Latin word *resilio* which means 'to bounce back.' It is defined as the capacity to recover from difficulties and to adapt successfully in the face of threats, fear, disasters, stress, and overwhelm. Resilience is our ability to persevere and adjust in times of adversity.

All children will face adversity of some sort, and trauma is often an inescapable fact of life. Trauma can result from events that are clearly extraordinary, such as violence, molestation, natural disasters, terrorism, serious illness, medical emergency, or death of a loved one. But children can also experience trauma from everyday, ordinary events such as changing schools, changing neighborhoods, not making the team, encountering bullies, medical procedures, and divorce. How our daughters deal with adversity and trauma, both minor and major, will have an impact on how successful and happy they are overall.

Thankfully, psychologists and social scientists have determined that resilience is a skill in which we all have access. Unlike eye color or height, resilience is not something we are either born with or not. Rather, resilience involves certain factors—certain behaviors, thoughts, and actions—that can be learned, developed, and fostered. The American Psychological Association reports the factors that contribute to resilience as:

1. Supportive relationships with family members, friends, and peers that build love and trust, provide nurturing, and offer encouragement and reassurance.

I am not what happened to me, I am what I choose to become.

Carl Jung

2. The ability to manage strong emotions.

3. A positive self-esteem and confidence in one's strengths and abilities.

4. Looking for positive meaning in one's life.

5. Practicing gratitude.

6. Maintaining a positive outlook.

Reading through this list, we see that the Heroines Club is a recipe for resilience! The Heroines Club is designed to build supportive relationships with family members, friends, and peers, and it supports our daughters in developing a positive self-esteem and confidence. Month two of the curriculum is specifically devoted to managing emotions, while month twelve encourages us to seek positive meaning in our lives. This month, then, our intention is to offer our daughters a potent dose of the final two ingredients needed for lifelong resilience in the face of whatever adversity—big or small—life throws their way: *gratitude* and a *positive attitude*.

Gratitude

Resilient people notice and appreciate the little, positive things, and find nourishment in the places that might easily be overlooked. Resilience requires making the choice to be grateful, despite the situation. It means asking yourself, "*What can I be grateful for right now?*" You see, thoughts of gratitude have the amazing power to lift our spirits and help us focus on what is still whole and enjoyable in life, all the while flooding our bodies with endorphins—the feel-good hormones. In over one hundred studies to date, researchers have found that people who have a daily gratitude practice consistently experience more positive emotions and demonstrate

Gratitude unlocks the fullness of life. It turns what we have into enough, and more. It turns denial into acceptance, chaos into order, and confusion into clarity. It can turn a meal into a feast, a house into a home, a stranger into a friend. Gratitude makes sense of our past, brings peace for today, and creates a vision for tomorrow.

Melody Beattie

— 127 —

psychological resilience. Learning to practice gratitude is one of life's most valuable lessons, and this month we set the intention to offer this important daily practice to our daughters.

Positive Attitude

Research shows that seeing the positive side of life experiences, learning from mishaps, and practicing positive thoughts leads to happier and more resilient children and adults. In his book, *The Optimistic Child*, researcher Martin E.P. Seligman, Ph.D., describes a thirty-year study in which he and his colleagues determined that positive thinking helps ward off depression and stress, improves school and work performance, and even improves physical health.

We are not talking about taking a 'Pollyanna' approach to life or adversity. Instead, striving to maintain a positive attitude is about looking at the situation realistically, searching for ways you can improve the situation, and trying to learn from your experiences.

Fortunately, like gratitude, a positive attitude can be taught, learned, and cultivated, even if you or your daughter tends toward pessimism or depression. In an effort to foster a positive attitude in ourselves and our daughters this month, we will become aware of the strong relationship between our thoughts and feelings and how we experience life, regardless of the external circumstances in which we may find ourselves.

Practicing the skills needed for lifelong resilience begins in childhood, and as mothers, we can foster these behaviors in our daughters. Life is full of suffering, but by instilling the habits needed for psychological resilience, we empower our daughters to not only survive, but to thrive.

May our daughters grow like the resilient willow tree, with strong, healthy roots, branches flexible enough to bend with the storm, and

Resilient people are characterized by an ability to experience both negative and positive emotions, even in difficult or painful situations. They mourn losses and endure frustrations, but they also find redeeming potential or value in most challenges. When not-so-resilient people face difficulties, all of their emotions turn negative. Resilient people, while they certainly see and acknowledge the bad, will find a way to also see the good.

Barbara Frederickson

firm enough to weather the strong winds of life without breaking.

We are in this together.

Love,
Melia

Getting to Know Our Heroine

Annelies Marie "Anne" Frank (1929–1945) was a Holocaust diarist and writer. She was born in Frankfurt, Germany, but her family decided to flee to Amsterdam when she was four years old because a dangerous man named Adolf Hitler had come into power as the head of the National Socialist, or Nazi, party. Anne's family was Jewish and Hitler hated Jewish people. He blamed them for all of Germany's problems and planned to kill them all. After fleeing to Amsterdam, the Frank family created a new life for themselves: Mr. Frank started a new company, Mrs. Frank took care of their new apartment and began building a community for their family, and Anne and her sister Margot started school. Anne liked to read, swim, ride her bike, ice-skate, and go to the movies with her friends.

In 1939, Hitler invaded Poland and World War II began. The Franks and other Jewish families hoped that Hitler would be defeated so they could safely return to their home country. Instead, in 1940, their worst fear came true: Germany invaded the Netherlands and there was no time and nowhere for the Frank family to run.

Life immediately changed once the Netherlands was occupied by the Nazis. All Jewish people were required to register with the Germans and turn over most of their money and their businesses. Each Jewish person over the age of six had to start wearing a big, yellow Star of David patch on their clothing to identify them.

Jewish people were no longer allowed in movie theaters, restaurants, libraries, beaches, pools, parks or hotels. They were forbidden to own cars or ride bikes and were restricted to a curfew. From 8pm–6am they had to remain indoors. Anyone caught disobeying the Nazis was arrested. Hitler's treatment of the Jews was wrong, unfair, and inhumane.

In June of 1942, Anne turned thirteen and received a most special birthday gift: a small notebook with a red and green checked cover that locked. It was in this diary, which she named "Kitty," that Anne recorded what would later become the most widely-read account of the Holocaust.

Shortly after receiving her diary, the Frank family received a notice in the mail that their oldest daughter, Margot, was to be sent to a labor camp in Germany. Sending their daughter to the Nazis was unthinkable for Mr. and Mrs. Frank. They knew that their only other choice was to do what many other Jewish people were doing: disappear into hiding. That night, the family left their apartment and most of their belongings and went to Mr. Frank's office building, where there was a secret stairway leading to a group of rooms. This "Secret Annex" is where Anne and her family lived until they were discovered and captured two years later.

Although Anne did not survive the war, her remarkable diary did. After her death, the diary was turned into a book that has since been translated into more than sixty-five languages and adapted for multiple plays and movies. Her diary has come to symbolize both the horrors of war and the amazing resilience of the human spirit.

Anne Frank remains an inspiration for women and girls today as a beacon of hope and an example of resilience amidst the most horrifying of circumstances. Among the many other wise and beautiful lessons we can learn from Anne Frank, she teaches us that attitude and gratitude do indeed have a tremendous impact on how one experiences life, regardless of the circumstances.

Discussion Prompts

1. *The Diary of Anne Frank* has become one of the world's most widely read works of non-fiction after the Bible. Why do you think Anne's diary and her story have attracted so much attention?

2. How do you think Anne maintained an attitude of hope and gratitude, even in the face of such horrible hardship and brutality?

3. Why do you think Mr. Frank's business colleagues were willing to risk their lives to help the Franks? Do you think you would have done the same if you were in their position?

4. Anne changed a lot in two years, as evident by her journal entries. Think about yourself two years ago—in what ways have you changed?

5. Do you have a diary or journal? What has been your experience with journaling?

6. If you had to live in hiding and could not make a sound all day, what would you do to occupy your mind and fill your time?

7. How might a positive attitude and a regular practice of gratitude contribute to resilience?

8. Who do you know among your family, friends, and community that exemplify resilience?

9. What does this month's affirmation, "I Am Resilient in the Face of Adversity," mean to you?

Integrated Activities

Pebble in My Shoe

SUPPLIES

◉ One small pebble for every circle participant

◉ Timer

INSTRUCTIONS

The Pebble in My Shoe activity illustrates the power of our attention and thoughts on our overall experience. Each circle member will place one small pebble in her shoe. As a circle, you will take two five-minute, silent walks around the space, or better yet, outside, if that is an option.

For the first walk, instruct the circle to focus on the pebble in their shoe—the way it feels, how it would feel without it, the way it impedes the experience, etc. For the second walk, instruct the circle to focus not on the pebble, but on the beauty around them. If your attention is pulled toward the annoying pebble, gently redirect your thoughts back toward the beauty around you.

After the two walks, remove the pebbles and place them on the altar around Anne's picture. Allow time for each mother and daughter to share their experience with this activity. Was it difficult to focus on the beauty around you with a pebble in your shoe? Were there things you did not notice in the first walk that you were able to see in the second? What did you learn from this activity?

Invite the circle to keep the pebble in their pocket as a symbol of everything in their lives that is good. When they feel low, they can touch the pebble and remind themselves that they have the resilience that is needed to survive any misfortune that life throws their way.

Gratitude Jar

◎ Jars—Mason jars or pickle jars work well. Enough for every mother-daughter pair to have one.

◎ Items to decorate the jar—ribbon, scrapbook paper, glue, stickers, markers, etc.

◎ Sheets of scrapbook paper—enough for every mother-daughter pair to have one sheet.

◎ Zip-lock plastic bags—enough for each mother-daughter pair to have one.

◎ Scissors

◎ Timer

INSTRUCTIONS

A Gratitude Jar is a fun way to provide a visual reminder of the many blessings in our lives. Sometimes it is the simplest things that make life wonderful and taking time to appreciate those moments of joy help you to cherish your life and yourself. On a down day, a quick glance at your Gratitude Jar will remind you that life is full of wonderful things to be grateful for and that you have the strength and support to overcome anything.

STEPS

1. Using the supplies provided, decorate your own jar to serve as a Gratitude Jar.

2. Cut the scrapbook paper into strips and place in a zip-lock bag.

3.   Take the Gratitude Jar and bag of paper strips home and place it in a communal area, such as in the kitchen or living room area.

4.   Each day, write at least one thing for which you are grateful, or that made you smile that day, on a slip of paper and place it in the jar. Help your daughter find the joy in everyday things—warm towels fresh from the dryer, a new book by her favorite author at the library, the full moon, the colorful evening sunset . . .

5.   At the end of each month, open the jar and read through the gratitude memories from that month together.

Allow time for each mother-daughter pair to share their Gratitude Jar creation and describe where they plan to keep it and how they plan to use it.

Medicine Meditation

Set your things to the side, find a comfortable, fully-supported resting position, perhaps take your mother's hand if that would feel good to you, and begin to follow your breath. In your mind's eye let's travel together to the Frank's Secret Annex. Anne is sitting at the small kitchen table with her sister and mother, peeling potatoes for tonight's dinner. The three women are smiling and enjoying each other's company and this sweet moment in time together. With playful warmth in her eyes, Anne offers you a seat with them at the table and hands you a potato and knife. As you begin to peel potatoes with the Frank women, what feelings are you having? Is there something you would like to ask Anne or the other women? Go ahead and ask her. Does Anne have a message for you? Listen to her. Offer gratitude to Anne for her life, her story and her resilience. Thank her for teaching you that a positive attitude and gratitude can be seeded in even the most awful circumstances. Thank you, Anne. As you look at Anne here in this moment, what words come to mind? What words or phrases describe the medicine of Anne Frank to you? When you are ready, send Anne your love and gratitude and gently open your eyes and return to our circle.

Quote Study

"I don't think of all the misery, but of all the beauty that still remains."

"Despite everything, I believe that people are really good at heart."

"Think of all the beauty still left around you and be happy."

"The best remedy for those who are afraid, lonely, or unhappy is to go outside, somewhere they can be quiet, alone with the heavens, nature, and God. Because only then does one feel that all is as it should be."

"How wonderful it is that nobody need wait a single moment before starting to improve the world."

"I know what I want, I have a goal, an opinion, I have a religion and love. Let me be myself and then I am satisfied. I know that I'm a woman, a woman with inward strength and plenty of courage."

Recommended Resources

Books for mothers and daughters, ages 7+

Anne Frank, by Poole, J.

Anne Frank: A Hidden Life, by Pressler, M.

Anne Frank: Beyond the Diary, by van der Rol, R. and Verhoeven, R.

A Friend Called Anne, by van Maarsen, J.

Who Was Anne Frank? by Abramson, A.

Books for mothers and daughters, ages 12+

Anne Frank: The Diary of a Young Girl, by Anne Frank

Anne Frank Remembered: The Story of Miep Gies, Who Helped Hide the Frank Family, by Gies, M.

Anne Frank: The Biography, by Mueller, M.

Anne Frank: A Photographic Story of a Life, by Knapp Sawyer, K.

Film

Anne Frank Remembered (1995)

The Diary of Anne Frank (2009)

Web

www.annefrank.org

www.annefrank.ch

www.youtube/annefrank

Additional Recommended Resources for Mothers

Rising Strong, by Brown, B.

The Gift of Failure: How the Best Parents Learn to Let Go So Their Children Can Succeed, by Lahey, J.

The Optimistic Child: A Proven Program to Safeguard Children Against Depression and Build Lifelong Resilience, by Seligman, M.

Trauma-Proofing Your Kids, A Parents' Guide for Instilling Confidence, Joy, and Resilience, by Levine, P. and Kline, M.

MARY CASSATT

"I Am Unconditionally Loved"

Dear Mothers,

May is the month of mother love. With the celebration of Mother's Day in the U.S., Canada and Australia, May offers us a potent and germane time to consider the love we share with our daughters. Our heroine this month, Mary Cassatt, was a gifted artist with a heart for feminism and a devotion to portraying the love between mothers and children in her work. Through getting to know this heroine, we will be inspired to explore the powerful and crucial bonds that exist between mother and daughter.

A few years ago, I was blessed to meet bestselling author Sue Monk Kidd and her then nineteen-year-old daughter, Ann Kidd Taylor while they were in Atlanta, Georgia promoting their highly-successful dual memoir, *Traveling with Pomegranates: A Mother-Daughter Story*. At this point in my life, the Heroines Club was a just tiny seed in my heart, and I was all-consumed with its growth and development. As I listened to Sue and Ann speak about their book and the writing process, what struck me most was the tender and connected dynamic the two of them shared. Their aura— the words they spoke, the ways they touched and looked at one another, the laughter they shared—all pointed to unconditional

A daughter's need for her mother is biologic, and it continues throughout her life. Not only was our mother's body the source of life for us, but it was her face that we looked to, to see how we were doing. By gazing into our mother's eyes and experiencing her response to us, we learned crucial first lessons about our own worth.

Christiane Northrup

love and mutuality. *That*, I thought, *is what we all want to have with our daughters!* I was enthralled! *How do we get what they have?* I wondered. When the floor was opened for questions from the audience, I was the first to jump from my seat and onto the stage. The question I most wanted answered by my favorite author was not about her writing, but about her mothering: "In your opinion, what do daughters most need from their mothers?" The audience chuckled at the magnitude of my question. Sue smiled thoughtfully and looked at Ann, the connection between them palpable. Turning back to me she said, "Unconditional love is a must. As long as a daughter knows—*really knows*—she is loved by her mother, she will be able to navigate the rest of her life much more easily." And then after a brief pause to reflect, Sue continued, "I remember staying up until 2am writing a letter to Ann the night before she left for college. In it, I told her to 'be true to herself' and to 'always err on the side of audacity.' We must empower our daughters to discover their being." With the kind of full-body chills that come when you know you are witnessing a divinely inspired moment, I offered my deepest gratitude and returned to my seat with the gift of her succinct words echoing in my heart: ***If our daughters are to be fully empowered to discover and develop their own, unique self, we as their mothers must offer them a firm foundation of unconditional love.*** The truth of her response was both freeing (love is all they need!) and daunting (how do we make sure our daughters know they are loved without conditions, especially for those of us who did not receive this kind of love from our own mothers?)

Loving Our Daughters

One way we can show our daughters our love is by being physically and emotionally available for tender moments of connection, like those depicted by Mary Cassatt in her art. As our daughters mature, these intimate moments often become more elusive and scattered, but as Dr. Christiane Northrup said, "A daughter's need for her mother is biologic, and continues throughout her life."

It is crucial that as our daughters grow, we continue to hold space for them to connect with us on a regular basis. By participating in the Heroines Club, you are already giving your daughter the vital gift of time to connect with you, both in circle with other mothers and daughters, and at home exploring the monthly recommended books and media resources together. Another easy and fun way to keep the mother-daughter connection strong and the lines of communication open is through sharing a journal, which we will create in circle this month as our Integrated Activity.

Unconditionally

To love our daughters unconditionally means that the love we offer them needs no prerequisites or criteria: she doesn't have to be anything, or do anything in particular to earn our love. Our love is unassailable and permanent. Our love is a given.

This month, with great compassion for yourself, I invite you to become aware of any conditions you may be inadvertently placing on your mother-love. Our daughters need to hear, both in words and in actions, "I love you because you are my daughter, and nothing you could ever do or not do could ever make me love you any less." This is the gift of unconditional love.

An old truism states that "we can't give what we don't have." For those of us that did not experience unconditional love from our

Try to see your child as a seed that came in a packet without a label. Your job is to provide the right environment and nutrients and to pull the weeds. You can't decide what kind of flower she will be or in what season she will bloom.

Anonymous

mothers (for whatever reasons), it can feel challenging to give that kind of love to our daughters. The good news is: it is never too late to receive the unconditional love that is your birthright. You can give it to yourself! As we explore mother love this month, I invite you to explore ways that you might begin mothering and loving yourself, unconditionally.

We are in this together.

Love,
Melia

Getting to know our heroine

Mary Stevenson Cassatt (1844–1926) was a painter and printmaker, and the first American Impressionist artist. She was born in Pennsylvania, but lived much of her adult life in France, where she befriended Edgar Degas and later exhibited among the Impressionists. At the time, female professional artists were rare, and paintings of mothers with children were not a common subject. Mary, however, created tender portrayals of the social and private lives of women, with particular emphasis on the intimate bonds between mothers and children. Her paintings strongly show the bond between mothers and daughters, and like all good art, her paintings helped people see the world, and themselves differently. At a time when women, mothers, and children were deeply undervalued by society, Mary exalted the power of the feminine through her art.

In the early 1900s, women were discouraged from pursuing an education or a career because it was seen as unnatural, inappropriate, and incompatible with a marriage and family. Mary's own parents objected to her becoming a professional artist for that reason. Even so, Mary, a self-possessed woman with strong character, dedicated herself to a career as an artist, and she boldly moved to Paris to join the newly developing Impressionist movement. Rather than focusing solely on accurate depictions, Impressionism sought to capture the *feeling* of a moment. This was very different to the art people were used to seeing and many thought it looked strange and flawed. Consequently, the early Impressionists were considered amateurs, and their work was shunned by powerful academic art institutions.

Nonetheless, Mary and the early Impressionists held true to their vision of art. Eventually their work was accepted, giving artists from that point on free rein to experiment. Mary continues to be an inspiration for girls and women today because of her stalwart dedication to her vision for her life and her art, even in the face of harsh judgment and ridicule, as well as her reverence for the sacred relationship between mothers and their children.

Discussion Prompts

1.   Mary Cassatt's visit home, long after she had achieved fame in Europe, was reported in the Philadelphia newspaper as, "the arrival of Mary Cassatt, sister of Mr. Cassatt, President of the Pennsylvania Railroad, who has been studying painting in France and owns the smallest Pekingese dog in the world." How do you think reading this introduction made Mary feel? Have you ever felt unseen or had your accomplishments minimized? Have you ever experienced your value being spoken of in terms of your relationship to a man? How did you handle that?

2.   Edgar Degas (a French Impressionist who loved to paint ballerinas) was an inspiration for Cassatt. Who has been an inspiration for you in your field or interest area?

3.   In Mary's day, most women did not work outside the home and raise children at the same time. Mary decided early in life that marriage would be incompatible with her career and she made sacrifices for her art; she had no husband or children and lived away from home. Do you think those sacrifices are still necessary today? Do you think women have to choose between motherhood and a career?

4.   From ancient times to today, women throughout the world have created amazing, beautiful, and revolutionary art. For the most part, however, women's artistic creations have been systematically excluded from the art establishment. Even today, less than 4% of the artists in the Modern Art Section of New York's Metropolitan Museum of Art are women, but 76% of the nude paintings feature women. Why do you think this is?

5.   Mary was especially drawn to painting women in everyday domestic settings, with special emphasis on the intimate bonds between mothers and children. What 'scene' might Mary have painted of you and your mother or daughter to represent your bond? When do you experience everyday bonding together?

6.   When you paint or draw, what is your favorite subject or focus? How do you feel when you create art?

7.   We give and receive love in many different ways. In his book, *The Five Love Languages of Children,* relationship counselor Gary Chapman identifies five primary love "languages" people speak. They are: Words of Affirmation, Quality Time, Receiving Gifts, Acts of Service, and Physical Touch. What do you think is your primary love "language"? When do you feel the most loved?

8.   What does *unconditional* love mean to you?

9.   How do you show your mother/daughter unconditional love?

10. How do you show *yourself* unconditional love?

11. What does this month's affirmation, "I am unconditionally loved," mean to you?

Integrated Activities

Creating Mother-Daughter Journals

Inspired by this month's affirmation, mothers and daughters will create a mother-daughter journal. A mother-daughter journal is a shared notebook or diary for letters, stories, doodles, and dreams to be passed between mother and daughter. Shared journaling is a way for us to show our daughters our unconditional love, acceptance, and support, and it offers our daughters an alternative approach to communicate any thoughts and questions they may feel too embarrassed or vulnerable to express verbally. This open communication is exactly what we want! In her book, *The Birth of Pleasure: A New Map of Love,* Carol Gilligan writes, "One confiding relationship, meaning where one can speak one's heart and mind freely, has been found to be the best protection against most forms of psychological trouble, especially in times of stress."

For their safety and overall well-being, we want our daughters to come to us for guidance when they are lost or hurting. Multiple safe channels of communication make the entire relationship more effective. The journal you create in circle this month will become a treasured mothering tool, allowing you to maintain a deep and healthy connection with your most beloved girl.

Supplies

◎ Journals. Any notebook will do, but I recommend something with a blank, heavy-duty writable cover for decorating and embellishing, with either plain or lined paper inside. Each mother/ daughter pair should have their own.

◎ Markers

◎ Glue sticks

◎ Decorative scrapbook paper, inspiring words and images (from magazines or printed from online), stickers, etc.

◎ Timer

Instructions

Take a few deep breaths, calming and opening your heart and mind to the creative journey about to unfold. This is a fun, uplifting activity and there is no wrong way to do it! You may choose to play soft, meditative music in the background, while encouraging mothers and daughters to share the experience by working alongside one another and conversing quietly. Set the timer for 30 minutes and announce when the last few minutes remain to make any finishing touches. After the allotted time is complete, clean the area and gather supplies. Hold space for each mother and daughter to share their decorated journal, while always welcoming anyone to "pass" if they would rather keep their creation private.

Steps

1. Using the art and craft supplies provided, decorate the front and back cover of your journal, perhaps writing this month's mantra as the title. Decorate your journal in any way that feels fun and positive for you.

2.   Together, decide on a dedicated place in your home, perhaps on your pillow or bedside table to show that there is a new message to read. Pass the journal back and forth between mother and daughter as desired.

Love Tanks

Inspired by Gary Chapman's book, *The Five Love Languages of Children*, this Integrated Activity will offer mothers and daughters a visual reminder of the many ways we give and receive love.

Inside every child is an 'emotional tank' waiting to be filled with love.

Gary Chapman

SUPPLIES

◎   Small plastic or glass jar, preferably heart-shaped, with a cork or lid. Enough for each mother-daughter pair to have one. Jars can be purchased at craft stores or online.

◎   Small sand art funnels. Enough for every mother-daughter pair to have one. Small funnels can be purchased at craft stores or online.

◎   Five different colors of craft sand. Enough for every mother-daughter pair to have a small amount of each color. Colored craft sand can be purchased in craft stores or online.

◎   Spoons. Enough for each mother-daughter pair to have one.

◎   A written or printed key explaining what each different color represents. For example: Green = Receiving Gifts, Pink = Physical Touch, Blue = Words of Affirmation, Yellow = Quality Time, and Orange = Acts of Service. Provide one copy of the key for each mother-daughter pair.

INSTRUCTIONS

1.   Remove the lid from the jar and place the small funnel into the top of the jar.

2.   Using the color key as your guide and the spoon provided, place a small amount of each color into the jar, creating a beautiful layered effect. Tap the jar gently to compact the sand in between each different layer.

3.   As the love tank jars are filled, discussion between mothers and daughters regarding the specific ways they give and receive love within their relationship is encouraged.

4.   Once filled, place the lid firmly on the jar.

5.   Together as mother and daughter, decide on a location in your home to place your special "love tank" as a reminder of this month's affirmation.

Medicine Meditation

Set your things to the side, find a comfortable, fully-supported resting position, perhaps take your mother's hand if that would feel good to you, and begin to follow your breath. In your mind's eye, travel back in time with me to Mary's art studio. She is there, surrounded by many of her masterpieces that you now recognize. Some of them are complete, while others are still in the early stages of development. You and your mother sit down together in a soft, comfortable blue chair across from Mary. Today, she is starting a new piece and you and your mother are her models. See the brush in her hand, as she carefully selects the perfect color from her palette and gently applies large strokes of paint onto the canvas. She has a message for you that she wants to express in her painting.

Mary glances at you and your mother, seated on the blue chair in front of her, and she smiles. What does the painting look like? What messages is she sending you? As she returns to her work, I invite you to think of a word or phrase that describes Mary, her life and her story. That word or phrase is part of the medicine that Mary offers us. Take a few more breaths, send your love back to her, and when you are ready, open your eyes.

Quote Study

"I think that if you shake the tree, you ought to be around when the fruit falls to pick it up."

"Women should be someone and not something."

"I have touched with a sense of art some people—they felt the love and the life. Can you offer me anything to compare to that joy for an artist?"

"I doubt if you know the effort it is to paint! The concentration it requires, to compose your picture, the difficulty of posing the models, of choosing the color scheme, of expressing the sentiment and telling your story. The trying and trying again and again and oh, the failures, when you have to begin all over again! The long months spent in effort upon effort; making sketch after sketch. Oh, my dear! No one but those who have painted a picture knows what it costs in time and strength!"

Recommended Resources

BOOKS FOR MOTHERS AND DAUGHTERS, AGE 7+

Mary Cassatt (Getting to Know the World's Greatest Artists), by Venezia, M.

Mary Cassatt: Impressionist Painter, by Harris, L.

BOOKS FOR MOTHERS AND DAUGHTERS, AGE 12+

I Always Loved You: A Novel, by Oliveria, R.

Mary Cassatt: A Life, by Matthews, N.

FILM FOR MOTHERS AND DAUGHTERS, AGE 7+

Mary Cassatt: An American Impressionist (1999)

WEB

www.biography.com/people/mary-cassatt-9240820

www.theartstory.org/artist-cassatt-mary.htm

ADDITIONAL RECOMMENDED RESOURCES FOR MOTHERS

Raise the Child You've Got – Not the One You Want: Why Everyone Thrives When Parents Lead With Acceptance, by Rose, N.

The Five Love Languages of Children, by Chapman, G.

How to Really Love Your Child, by Campbell, R.

Unconditional Parenting: Moving from Rewards and Punishment to Love and Reason, by Kohn, A.

JANE GOODALL

"I Listen to My Intuition"

There is no greater blessing a mother can give her daughter than a reliable sense of the veracity of her own intuition. Intuition is handed down from parent to child in the simplest of ways: 'You have good judgment. What do you think lies hidden behind all this?'

Rather than defining intuition as some unreasoned faulty quirk, it is defined as truly the soul speaking. Intuition senses the direction to go in for most benefit, it is self-preserving, has a grasp of underlying motive and intention, it chooses what will cause the least amount of fragment to the psyche . . .

This intuitive function belongs to all women. It is a massive and fundamental receptivity. Not receptivity as once touted in classical psychology that is a passive vessel, but receptivity as in possessing immediate access to a profound wisdom that reaches to women's very bones.

Dr. Clarissa Pinkola Estes

Dear Mothers,

This month, Jane Goodall reminds us to give our daughters (and ourselves!) a most important gift: the permission and encouragement to tune in to, listen, and trust our intuition. Having a strong connection with their intuition will keep our daughters safer and support them in making decisions that are in alignment with their highest good. Dr. Jane Goodall is the perfect heroine to guide us on our journey this month! Her life and work are living testaments to the beauty and wisdom that comes when we listen to our intuition.

What is intuition?

Often referred to as a "gut feeling," "instinct," "inner voice" or "sixth sense," intuition is a deep, brilliant, protective and powerful force within us all. Our intuition comes from our body's desire to keep us safe and thriving. It is the ability to understand something immediately, without the need for conscious reasoning; it is the knowing/sensing of something beyond time, space, reason, the active use of prior knowledge or the five senses. Through our intuition, we tap into our subconscious minds, which is where we "archive" all kinds of information that we don't necessarily remember or know on a conscious level. Acting as her first mate up in the crow's nest of her ship, learning to listen to her inner voice of intuition will allow your daughter to see far ahead and know which direction to steer herself for the greatest safety and fulfillment.

Our intuition communicates with us in myriad ways, such as physical and emotional feelings, dreams, flashes of insight, synchronicities, or visions in nature. For example, when your body feels threatened, you may get a "gut reaction" that feels like a tightening in your stomach, or perhaps your breathing becomes shallower. When making a decision, you might notice that as you consider your options, one choice in particular makes your heart feel more expansive than the other choices. Or perhaps you receive insight from dreams, awaking and simply *knowing* what to do. Chances are, your intuition probably takes multiple different forms, and over time, your daughter and you will come to know your intuition's favorite way to get your attention. The often quiet source of inner wisdom is always communicating: it is our job to *listen*.

Cultivating Intuition

First, let me say that intuition is a natural process and you do not have to work hard to discover its gifts. Simply inviting intuition into your life as you would a dear friend, staying alert to your intuition's communication, and welcoming it with a sense of gratitude and joy is all that is really necessary to cultivate intuition.

If the idea of intuition is a new concept for your daughter, begin by setting aside some quality time this month to explicitly explain intuition and give her the vocabulary to discuss it.

Like a muscle, intuition gets stronger the more you use it. The following activities can be shared together at home to cultivate your daughter's intuition.

Guiding Questions

A potent time to communicate the value of inner guidance is when our daughters have decisions to make, or they come to us with a problem or concern. Rather than immediately going into problem-solver or advice-giver mode, discuss the situation with your daughter, asking her guiding questions to get her in touch with her intuition, such as:

"What is your intuition telling you about this?"

"What would that be like?"

"If you could wave a magic wand, what would you create?"

"What feels right to you?"

Communicate Your Own Intuitional Insights

As with everything else, our daughters learn best from our model. Consider using language such as:

"My intuition is telling me . . . "

"It feels right to . . . "

"My inner voice says . . . "

Meditate

In a peaceful environment, find a comfortable and fully-supported resting position, close your eyes and begin to pay attention to your breath. Focus only on the air as it moves into your body, filling your lungs, and then as it moves back up and out. If your mind starts to wander, that's okay; gently bring your attention back to your breath. This is a wonderful daily practice to teach your daughter, for even just five minutes of meditation can help quiet the brain's chatter and create space for intuition to flourish.

Eat intuitively

Practice listening to your body's inner wisdom by respecting its cues around hunger: eat when you are hungry and stop when you have had enough. Rather than thinking about what you *should* eat, listen to what your body truly *wants* to feel good and nourished and encourage your daughter to do the same. I know this is easier said than done for many of us raised in the current culture. If this is an area where you struggle, I highly recommend the life-changing book, *Intuitive Eating*, by Evelyn Tribole and Elyse Resch.

Welcome all feelings

Having an authentic awareness and connection with your feelings is required for intuition to function at its full capacity. We discussed emotional intelligence and the healthy expression of all feelings in the chapter about Frida Kahlo, but it is also important to note here because of how important feelings are to intuition: feelings let us know about needs. Rather than distracting or stuffing them down, we want our girls to be aware of, and informed by, their feelings. To support this, show your daughter that it is okay to experience the full range of emotions by honoring the healthy expressions of all feelings, even the less pleasant ones. When big emotions visit our home, I often remember the beautiful poem "The Guest House" written by 13th century poet and mystic, Rumi, which begins:

This being human is a guest house. Every morning a new arrival.

A joy, a depression, a meanness, some momentary awareness comes as an unexpected visitor.

Welcome and entertain them all!

Journal about and discuss your dreams

Place a journal and pen on your daughter's and your bedside tables. Before going to sleep at night, ask your inner self to offer you a dream or image that will nourish and guide you. When you wake up, write about, or draw pictures of, your dreams. If you can't remember the specific details, record your general feelings and impressions upon waking. Spending time with your daughter looking over and pondering your dreams can be a playful and bonding way to cultivate intuition. What messages might your intuition be communicating to you through your dreamtime?

Spend time in nature

As studying the life and work of heroine Jane Goodall teaches us, cultivating intuition requires *presence* and *observation*, and there is no better place to practice these skills than in nature! Jane was of the mindset that humans are a part of nature and should return to their roots in order to solve problems. Following your intuition, chose a spot in nature to sit quietly, and then wait and observe the world around you. What sounds do you hear? What animals or insects emerge? What life lessons or insights do you see reflected in the natural world?

Take an 'intuition walk'

Go for a walk outside and rely solely on your intuition to guide which route you take. If you feel called to go left, go left! When turning right feels right, do it! Rather than planning a route, let your intuition guide each step of the way. How does it feel to follow your intuition? What do you observe on your walk? Are there any "gifts"—such as finding a feather or meeting an old friend—which you wouldn't have experienced had you not taken this particular route?

This month, we are teaching our daughters (and reminding ourselves) that we have a wise source *within* that we can call upon at any time for answers and guidance. The intuitive life is one of confidence, inner peace, and creative expression. What an amazing gift, indeed!

We are in this together.

Love,
Melia

Getting to Know Our Heroine

Valerie "Jane" Morris-Goodall (born April 3, 1934) is a world famous scientist and outspoken animal rights champion. She is most famous for her detailed forty-five-year study of the social and family interactions of wild chimpanzees in Gombe Stream National Park, Tanzania. Jane's work with wild chimpanzees represents one of the world's greatest scientific achievements, as it forever changed the way we view the animal kingdom and ultimately ourselves.

Rain or shine, Jane followed her intuition and crawled through tangled vines, climbed trees, and sat for hours, quietly waiting and watching with a calm attentiveness. She kept a journal from that time that now amounts to a masterpiece of laboriously recorded, precise detail. Her revolutionary discoveries proved to the world how alike humans and chimpanzees are. She discovered that chimps created and used tools, were omnivorous, had unique personalities and expressed emotions. She was the first to observe that chimps use different vocalizations (grunts, pants and screams) to communicate different things to one another. Unlike most researchers, Jane named the animals that were part of her studies. Flo, Olly, William and David Graybeard were a few of the names she gave to the chimps, based on their personalities or physical characteristics. Normally scientists assign numbers to the subjects, rather than names, in order to remove the possibility of becoming attached to them. Jane's scientific approach was unique and received much attention, and sometimes even criticism. Even so, Jane listened to and followed her intuition, showing the world what science can look like when head combines with heart.

Today, Jane travels three hundred days a year, giving lectures, meeting conservationists, pouring her energy into her chimp sanctuaries and the environmental youth movement she founded. Highly intuitive, empathic and in-tune with nature, Jane continues to be an inspiration to women and girls alike.

Discussion Prompts

1.   As a girl, Jane loved animals and just knew that someday she would go to Africa to study them in the wild. What is something in your life that you have always just *known*?

2.   One of her favorite toys as a child was a toy chimpanzee her father had given her after a baby chimp was born at the local zoo. What was/is your favorite childhood toy? Do you still have it? What meaning does it have for you?

3.   Jane had a beautiful beech tree in her childhood garden that she would climb and spend hours in. Where in nature do you most like to spend time and why?

4.   Jane spent her late teens and early twenties saving money to go to Africa. She worked various jobs, including as a secretary and a waitress. What was your first job? What is something you are saving money for?

5.   Jane's mother always encouraged her daughter to listen to her intuition and pursue her dreams. Growing up, she told Jane, "If you really want something, and if you work hard, take advantage of the opportunities, and never give up, you will somehow find a way." In 1960, African officials were concerned about the safety of Jane living alone among wild animals at Gombe Stream. They refused to let her go! They finally agreed when Jane's mother, not wanting her daughter to miss this amazing opportunity, offered to travel and stay with her. They spent four wonderful months in Africa together, mother supporting daughter. How does/did your mother support you in pursuing your dreams?

6.   Jane believed that watching the chimps taught her a lot about good mothering and later influenced how she cared for her own son. Who (or what) has had an influence on your mothering?

7. When asked in a 2010 interview, Jane named her mother and grandmother as her personal heroines. Who are your heroes and heroines?

8. In what ways and how does your intuition "speak" to you?

9. Was there a time when you listened to, trusted, and followed your intuition and you are glad that you did? Or a time that you didn't and wish you had?

10. What does this month's affirmation, "I Listen to My Intuition," mean to you?

Integrated Activities

Doodle Art

Inspired by this month's affirmation, mothers and daughters will tap into their intuition by creating doodle art together. Doodle art is a great way to strengthen your intuitive connection with yourself, as it is a wordless activity that is more felt than understood.

SUPPLIES

◎ Paper—enough for each mother and daughter to have their own piece.

◎ Colored markers

◎ Timer

Pass out the paper and markers. Take a few deep breaths, calming and opening your heart and mind to the creative journey about to unfold. This is a fun, uplifting activity and there is no wrong way to do it! You may choose to play soft, meditative music in the background, but encourage the circle to not talk to one another, as intuition requires *listening*.

Set a timer for 15 minutes and just begin putting the marker to paper. Start making marks automatically and quickly, without thought, allowing spontaneous images to take shape. See if your doodle shapes want to become a face, or a body, an animal, or a scene. You may want to emphasize certain areas as you allow loose, flowing movement with your marker. Allow your feelings to move into your hand and through your marker. Turn off the "censor" or "critic" within you and just keep your hand moving. Your doodle art may be simple or elaborate, abstract or representational. That's the beauty of it! Art is an expression of the individual and there is no 'right' way to do it. Give warning when time is nearly up so everyone can make their finishing touches.

After the allotted time is complete, clean the area, and gather supplies. Hold space for each mother and daughter to share her creation and give voice to her experience with intuitive doodling, always welcoming anyone to "pass" if they would rather keep their creation and thoughts private.

Encourage the circle to display their art somewhere they will see it often, as a reminder of this month's affirmation.

Find the Chimp

Supplies

◉ One small stuffed chimpanzee

Instructions

Inspired by Jane Goodall, Find the Chimp is a fun intuition-building game.

Sit in a circle with a small stuffed chimpanzee in the middle. One person leaves the room and another person in the circle places the toy chimp behind her back. The person comes back and uses intuition to determine who has the toy chimp. If she hasn't guessed correctly after three turns, the location is lovingly revealed. The game continues until everyone that wishes to has had a turn being the "finder."

Medicine Meditation

Set your things to the side, find a comfortable, fully-supported resting position, perhaps take your mother's hand if that would feel good to you, and begin to follow your breath. Let's travel together to Africa, where Jane is observing a community of chimpanzees. She is crouched down in the tall grass, looking through a pair of binoculars. She sees us quietly approaching and silently waves us over with a smile. Excitedly, she hands you her binoculars and encourages you to look through them at the scene she has already been watching for hours. What do you see? What message or lesson does this vision offer you? Take a breath and allow your heart to absorb this medicine. When you are ready, carefully hand the binoculars back to Jane, and offer her your love and gratitude. As you continue looking at Jane in your mind's eye, what word or phrase comes to mind for you? How might you describe the powerful medicine of Jane Goodall? Let's take a deep, cleansing breath together to seal this in, and when you are ready, open your eyes.

Quote Study

"Change happens by listening and then starting a dialogue with the people who are doing something you don't believe is right."

"The greatest danger to our future is apathy."

"The least I can do is speak out for those who cannot speak for themselves."

"Only if we understand can we care. Only if we care will we help. Only if we help shall they be saved."

"Every individual matters. Every individual has a role to play. Every individual makes a difference."

"Women tend to be more intuitive, or to admit to being intuitive, and maybe the hard science approach isn't so attractive. The way that science is taught is very cold. I would never have become a scientist if I had been taught like that."

Recommended Resources

Books for Mothers and Daughters Ages 7+

Who is Jane Goodall? by Edwards, R.

My Life with the Chimpanzees, by Jane Goodall

The Watcher: Jane Goodall's Life with the Chimps, by Winter, J.

Books for Mothers and Daughters Age 12+

Through a Window: My Thirty Years with the Chimpanzees of Gombe, by Jane Goodall

Jane Goodall: A Biography, by Greene, M.

Film

Among the Wild Chimpanzees (1987)

Jane Goodall's Wild Chimpanzees (2002)

Jane's Journey (2010)

Jane Goodall: to the Children on the Environment (2015)

Web

The Jane Goodall Institute, www.janegoodall.org

Jane Goodall's Roots & Shoots, www.rootsandshoots.org

Ted Talks, www.ted.com/speakers/jane_goodall

ADDITIONAL RECOMMENDED RESOURCES FOR MOTHERS

The Intuitive Spark: Bringing Intuition Home to Your Child, Your Family, and You, by Choquette, S.

Protecting the Gift: Keeping Children and Teenagers Safe (and Parents Sane), by de Becker, G.

Raising Intuitive Children: Guide Your Child to Know and Trust Their Gifts, by Goode, C.

HELEN KELLER AND ANNE SULLIVAN

"I Advocate for Myself"

Dear Mothers,

One of the most important skills we can teach our daughters, starting in childhood, is how to be comfortable advocating for themselves. Whether it is at home, in the community, in school, or someday in the workplace, our daughters need to know that it is their right—and their *responsibility*—to self-advocate. Our daughters need to know that it is okay to ask for what they want and need in a direct, respectful manner, and we can teach them how to do so.

The truth is, you can't always be there to advocate on your daughter's behalf, nor would you necessarily want to. As the old proverb states, "give a man a fish and you feed him for a day; teach a man to fish and you feed him for a lifetime." By teaching our daughters to advocate for themselves we are supporting their lifelong success and well-being in every domain of their lives.

And really, who better to represent your daughter's desires, goals, and beliefs than herself? Inspired by the exemplary model of our heroines this month, let us explore the idea of what it means to be your own best advocate.

You get in life what you have the courage to ask for.

Oprah Winfrey

What is self-advocacy?

The term *self-advocacy*, though initially associated with a civil-rights movement for individuals with disabilities, is more commonly defined today as **the ability to recognize, understand, and effectively communicate your wants and needs to others**. Self-advocacy is an important skill for all people: disabled, and non-disabled alike.

As a self-advocate, you are actively involved in getting what you want and need by speaking up for yourself, making your own decisions, standing up for your rights, and requiring that others treat you with respect.

Someone who self-advocates:

◎ says what they think and feel

◎ speaks up for the things they believe in

◎ knows and understands their rights and responsibilities

◎ takes responsibility for their own life

◎ makes decisions that affect their own life

◎ helps improve their life

◎ tries to change the way things are done

Teaching your daughter to advocate for herself

Learning to communicate what is important to us is a skill that can be practiced and learned. It is never too early to start helping your daughter become comfortable speaking up for herself. To help cultivate self-advocacy skills in your daughter, consider the following strategies:

◎ **Support her efforts to self-advocate.** Remind your daughter that she can always come to you for guidance and support, and that you will always be on her side and help her to work things out. When she does come to you with a problem or issue, rather than immediately jumping into problem-solver or rescuer mode, consider if it may be an opportunity for her to practice advocating for herself. Ask empowering questions and explore options with her rather than telling her how to solve it, and then support her in communicating on her own behalf, stepping in only if necessary.

◎ **Demonstrate, model, and practice assertive communication.** Assertiveness is a skill that takes practice. People who are assertive can express their desires with healthy confidence, while respecting the rights of others. They don't beat around the bush or expect people to read their minds. If something is bothering them, they speak up; if they want or need something, they ask. Assertive communicators know that it never hurts to ask, and in fact, it often helps. Model self-advocacy for your daughter in your own life; practice assertive communication within the family, with co-workers, neighbors, sales people, etc. You can teach and practice assertive communication directly by coming up with different scenarios where your daughter may need to be assertive (such as asking a teacher for help) and doing a few role-plays. Emphasize assertive posture, appropriate eye contact, assertive phrases, and a firm-sounding tone.

◎ **Offer her practice in the real-world.** Have your daughter order for herself at restaurants, ask the clerk at a store for help, ask for directions, make purchases and returns, ask questions at her own medical and dental appointments, and attend parent-teacher conferences when appropriate. Every day provides opportunities for your daughter to practice advocating for herself.

The truth is, self-advocacy can be hard. I work with many smart, competent, successful women who are great advocates for others, yet have difficulty transferring that skill to their own lives. Like many of the women I work with, you may find that you have difficulty asking for what you want and need, or asking for help, in your personal life. There are many reasons for this, but as women, we are relearning together that it is not only okay to express our wants and needs and make requests of others, but that doing so is both our right and our responsibility as the stewards of our own lives.

This month, as you explore the concept of self-advocacy with your daughter, I encourage you to consider your own experience as well: *what areas of your own life might benefit from more self-advocating?* Remember, we are the creators of our own lives, and as heroine Dr. Maya Angelou once said, "The wisest thing we can do is be on our own side."

We are in this together.

Love,
Melia

Getting to Know Our Heroines

Johanna "Anne" Mansfield Sullivan Macy (1866–1936) was an American teacher and pioneer in the field of education, best known for being the instructor and lifelong companion of Helen Keller.

Anne had a difficult start to life. Born in Agawam, Massachusetts, Anne and her siblings grew up in extreme poverty and struggled with health problems. At five years old, Anne contracted an eye disease called trachoma, which left her with severe vision loss. Anne's mother died of tuberculosis when Anne was only eight years old. After her mother's death, her father abandoned the children, leaving Anne and her brother Jimmie to be sent to live in a home for the poor called the Tewksbury Almshouse. The living conditions at the house were deplorable, and Jimmie, who was already medically fragile, died within three months of their arrival. Anne was devastated.

While at Tewksbury, Anne underwent several eye operations that gave her limited, short-term relief. At some point, she learned from another resident who was blind, about schools for the blind. Anne knew that her best hope to escape poverty was an education, and she knew she would have to advocate for herself to make it happen. In 1880 she had a chance to do just that.

A commission had come to Tewksbury to investigate the conditions. Anne followed the team of inspectors around, waiting for an opportunity to speak up for herself. Just as the tour was concluding, Anne gathered up all of her courage, approached a member of the group, and told him that she wanted to go to school. That moment of self-advocating changed Anne's life. On October 7, 1880, Anne Sullivan entered the Perkins School for the Blind (later called the Perkins Institute.)

Anne arrived at Perkins not knowing how to read or even write her name, but through self-advocacy, hard work, and determination, she not only graduated six years later, but she gave the Valedictory address!

Around the time of Anne's graduation, one thousand miles south in the small town of Tuscumbia, Alabama, a little girl named Helen Keller was turning six years old.

Helen Adams Keller (1880–1968) was a best-selling American author, political activist, international lecturer, and the first American deaf and blind person to graduate from college.

Helen began her life as a typically-developing, bright, and happy child. Then, when she was two years old, Helen became very sick. She ran an extremely high fever for many days and the doctors did not think she would survive. Helen did survive the terrible illness, but as her health recovered, it became clear to her parents that their beloved daughter could no longer see nor hear. The illness had left

Helen deaf, blind, and mute.

Over time, Helen found ways to communicate with those around her by using made-up signals to tell people what she wanted. For example, pulling on someone meant "come with me," and shoving them away meant she wanted them to go. By the time Helen was five years old, she had created over fifty of her own signs! Even still, Helen had tremendous difficulty communicating her wants and needs, and was frequently misunderstood. These misunderstandings often provoked terrible emotional outbursts by Helen, which frightened and concerned her parents. Helen was growing into an angry, rebellious, and isolated child. Helen's parents knew they needed help reaching and raising their daughter. The Kellers decided to seek out the advice of Alexander Graham Bell, inventor of the telephone and advocate for the deaf. He suggested that they contact the Perkins Institute for the Blind in Boston, Massachusetts. The director of the Perkins Institute recommended the intelligent and determined Ms. Anne Sullivan to serve as a personal governess for Helen.

Anne and Helen Meet

The meeting of these two powerful women can only be described as divine providence. In fact, Helen later referred to the day she first met Anne as her "soul's birthday." Anne unlocked a whole new world for Helen. She taught Helen to communicate with sign language, and to read, write, and even speak! With dedication and love, the twenty-year-old teacher broke through Helen's isolation, helping her to blossom as she learned to communicate.

In the early 1900s, few women went to college and no deaf-blind woman had ever completed college. Helen was a strong self-advocate, and she knew she could do it. With the help of her beloved teacher Anne, Helen attended one of the top women's universities in the United States, Radcliff College, and graduated with honors!

Helen became famous for her unprecedented achievements despite her disabilities. She used her fame to advocate not only for herself, but for the rights of all people with disabilities. She traveled to over forty countries giving speeches, wrote twelve books, and worked for the American Foundation for the Blind. Through it all, the wise and strong Anne Sullivan remained at Helen's side as her interpreter and constant companion.

The extraordinary story of Helen Keller and Anne Sullivan continues to inspire women and girls today as a symbol of courage and determination in the face of overwhelming odds, and as a reminder that we are always our own best advocates.

Discussion Prompts

1. Helen later described the day she first met Anne Sullivan as her "soul's birthday." What do you think she meant by that? Have you ever met someone or experienced something that made you feel like a part of your soul was being born or coming to life?

2. Helen starred in a movie about her life story. The film's title was *Deliverance*, which means "the state of being saved from something dangerous or unpleasant." Why do you think that name was chosen for the title? If there was a movie made about your life, what would be a fitting title?

3. Not being able to hear or see, Helen could only use her sense of touch, smell, and taste to experience the world. How do you experience the world through your five senses? Is one of your senses especially sensitive? Do you think one is stronger than the others?

4. Helen loved to be outdoors, so most of her lessons with Anne were outside. Where do you most enjoy being and learning?

5.   Do you know anyone who has overcome a handicap?

6.   What does self-advocacy mean to you and why do you think it is important?

7.   Think of someone you know who is a good self-advocate. What is their tone of voice? How do they stand? Do they make eye contact? What else do you notice?

8.   What are some ways you advocate for yourself?

9.   Have you had an experience where you did not advocate for yourself and later wished that you had? What did you learn from that experience?

10.   Is it ever selfish to advocate for yourself?

11.   What does this month's affirmation, "I Advocate for Myself" mean to you?

Integrated Activities

Sense of Touch Guess Bag

SUPPLIES

◎   Brown paper bags—enough for every mother-daughter pair to have one.

◎   6–8 small objects per mother daughter pair.

◎   Scarves or other blindfolds—enough for every mother-daughter pair to have one.

The Sense of Touch Guess Bag is a fun way to imagine how it might have felt for Helen to "see" the world through her sense of touch. Before circle, fill each paper bag with 6–8 items of varying texture, size, shape, and weight. Example items could be: a paperclip, dandelion flower, seed packet, potato, paintbrush, keychain, feather, and a coin. The bag's contents should differ from one another, so that each bag is unique. Mothers and daughters will pair up and take turns blindfolding one another and reaching into the bag. Using only your sense of touch, see if you can identify the objects in the bag. When you think you know what it is, pull it out and see if you were correct! After the activity is complete, allow time for mothers and daughters to share their experience with the Guess Bag. What was easy to identify? What was more difficult? What did you learn from this experience?

Self-Advocacy Interview

◉ Print off the following "interview questions" and provide a copy for each mother-daughter pair:

What do you want to learn or work on this year?

What are your special concerns when it comes to learning?

How do you learn best?

What do you need to be successful?

What would make learning easier for you?

What do you wish your teacher would understand about you?

How can you advocate for yourself as a learner?

◎ Pens

◎ Clipboards or other flat writing surface

To advocate for your wants and needs, you must first know what those wants and needs are. The Self-Advocacy Interview is a fun circle activity designed to help your daughter get clear on what her wants and needs are in an educational setting, as well as have an opportunity to practice advocating for herself.

INSTRUCTIONS

Mothers and daughters will pair up with a copy of the interview questions. Mothers will ask the daughters the self-advocacy interview questions, while scaffolding for responses and encouraging discussion. Mothers are invited to record their daughter's responses on the paper. After the allotted time is complete, allow mothers and daughters an opportunity to share any important ideas or insights gleaned from this activity.

Medicine Meditation

Set your things to the side, find a comfortable, fully-supported resting position, perhaps take your mother's hand if that would feel good to you, and begin to follow your breath. In your mind's eye, let's travel together to Radcliff College, where Helen is attending school. It is a beautiful, warm evening, and we are walking across the campus. We see Helen and Anne sitting together on a blanket under a big oak tree. The two women are studying together. Helen is reading a book written in Braille, while Anne is taking notes. Anne notices you approaching, and closing her book, invites you over to join them on the blanket. When you feel comfortable and ready, offer Helen your hand. What message does Helen have for you? Receive her words as they are lovingly spelled into your hand and thank her for teaching you the importance of self-advocacy. As you look at Helen and Anne here in this moment, what words come to mind? What words or phrases describe the medicine of Helen Keller and Anne Sullivan to you? When you are ready, send them your love and gratitude and gently open your eyes and return to our circle.

Quote Study

"The best and most beautiful things in the world cannot be seen or even touched—they must be felt with the heart."

"When one door of happiness closes, another opens; but often we look so long at the closed door that we do not see the one which has been opened for us."

"Optimism is the faith that leads to achievement. Nothing can be done without hope and confidence."

"What we have once enjoyed we can never lose. All that we love deeply becomes a part of us."

"Never bend your head. Always hold it high. Look the world straight in the eye."

"Self-pity is our worst enemy and if we yield to it, we can never do anything wise in this world."

Helen Keller

"Children require guidance and sympathy far more than instruction."

"A strenuous effort must be made to train young people to think for themselves and take independent charge of their lives."

"Don't be afraid to fail. Don't waste energy trying to cover up failure. Learn from your failures and go on to the next challenge. It's okay to fail. If you're not failing, you're not growing."

Anne Sullivan

Recommended Resources

BOOKS FOR MOTHERS AND DAUGHTERS, AGES 7+

Helen Keller: Courage in the Dark, by Hurwitz, J.

Who Was Helen Keller? by Thompson, G.

Helen Keller, by Davidson, M.

BOOKS FOR MOTHERS AND DAUGHTERS, AGES 12+

The Story of My Life, by Helen Keller

Miss Spitfire: Reaching Helen Keller, by Miller, S.

Helen Keller's Teacher, by Davidson, M.

FILM

The Miracle Worker (2000, also a theatrical play)

Deliverance (1919)

WEB

https://www.youtube.com/user/IamHelenKeller/videos

http://braillebug.afb.org/hkmuseum.asp

ADDITIONAL RESOURCES FOR MOTHERS

The Curse of the Good Girl: Raising Authentic Girls with Courage and Confidence, by Simmons, R.

Nonviolent Communication: A Language of Life: Life-Changing Tools for Healthy Relationships, by Rosenberg, M.

MALALA YOUSAFZAI

"I Am Worthy"

Dear Mothers,

This month's heroine and affirmation remind us of the plight our sisters around the world are facing in countries where gender inequality is at its most extreme—where "it's a girl" are the three deadliest words that can be spoken.

The mistreatment and abuse of half the world's population is the greatest moral issue of our time. According to the United Nations Institute for Statistics:

Your crown has been bought and paid for. Put it on your head and wear it.

Maya Angelou

 62 million girls across the world are out of school.

 Every year, 15 million girls are forced or coerced into marriage.

 150 million girls under eighteen have experienced rape or other forms of sexual violence.

 The leading cause of death for young women aged 15–19 in developing countries is pregnancy.

 200 million girls in the world today are missing.

 Unwanted female babies are aborted, killed, or abandoned in almost every continent in the world. Girls that survive infancy live a second-class life compared to their brothers, who are favored when

shelter, food, and medicine are scarce.

◎ In some parts of the world, women who do not produce sons are beaten, raped, or killed.

These statistics reflect the fact that, globally, girls and women are seen as *fundamentally unworthy*: unworthy of education and power, of health and body sovereignty, of freedom and independence, of safety and protection, of life.

Our heroine this month, Malala Yousafzai, describes her birth with the words, "When I was born, some of our relatives came to our house and told my mother, 'Don't worry, next time you will have a son.' I was a girl in a land where rifles are fired in celebration of a son, while daughters are hidden away behind a curtain, their role in life simply to prepare food and give birth to children." One can imagine the impact early experiences like this have on a girl's sense of self-worth.

When my daughter Della was born, her father and I cried deep, heartfelt tears of joy upon meeting our third child. Our family and community embraced us with celebration and thanksgiving. I remember nursing Della in the early morning light of that first day together, feeling so blessed, *so incredibly blessed*. I stroked her small cheek, looked deeply into her newborn eyes, and fell madly, eternally in love. As Della fell asleep in my arms, my thoughts turned to all the other baby girls born around the world that same day, and it was my hope that in rejoicing over Della's female existence, the vibration for girls everywhere would be raised; that they too would feel loved and worthy.

In the same way, it is my hopeful belief that today, by raising our daughters to claim their *fundamental, unchanging* worth as human beings, we make it that much more possible for their sisters all over the world to do the same. As Dr. Jean Shinoda Bolen once wrote, "An idea whose time has come depends upon a critical number of people embracing a new way of thinking, feeling, or perceiving.

Once that critical number is reached, what had been resisted becomes accepted. What was once unthinkable is then adopted by more and more people until it reaches a critical mass, and then becomes a commonly held standard of belief or behavior." May our lives and our mothering serve as the tipping point for the healing of girls and women everywhere.

What is self-worth?

Worthy: (adjective) *having high worth; deserving of attention and respect.*

Self-worth is a difficult concept to grasp; it is a function of how you value yourself. Unlike self-esteem, which is a person's sense of approval of herself—and can periodically fluctuate due to external circumstances or events—self-worth is a deep and unshakable belief in one's inherent value. This knowing is not dependent on anything other than a girl or woman's ability to say "I am," and to know that this statement, and indeed her very existence, is enough. Self-worth is valuing oneself, and respecting the fact that you were created with intrinsic value. A good sense of self-worth is the foundation of our ability to believe in ourselves, to care for ourselves, to advocate for ourselves, and to love ourselves.

What would you do if you knew you were worthy?

India Arie

A lack of self-worth can, and most often does, result in depression and self-destructive coping strategies. A lack of self-worth means that feelings of shame are present on a deep level. When a person with low self-worth makes a mistake, which we all do in life, instead of her inner voice telling her that she made a mistake, her inner voice tells her that she is a mistake. There is a big difference here, and in order to protect our daughters from depression, self-mutilation, eating disorders, and suicide, we must instill in them an unshakable sense of self-worth. When they don't make the team, aren't invited to the party, fail the test, or receive the college rejection letter, we want our daughters to know that regardless of how they "stack up" in life, they are still 100% worthy: worthy of love, of connection, of respect, of self-care, of failing and trying again, of receiving anything they desire.

This month, let us teach our daughters:

◎ The world doesn't get to tell you when to feel good about yourself.

◎ Everyone has different gifts and challenges. You can feel good about yourself no matter what your gifts and challenges are.

◎ Your worth is already established; it is not determined by looking or acting a certain way.

◎ You already have infinite worth and that does not change based on external factors.

By instilling a strong sense of self-worth in our daughters, we are offering them the gift of lifelong resiliency in the face of whatever challenges come their way. We are teaching them that they are worthy of **not accepting the unacceptable** in terms of relationships, jobs, and treatment by others. We are teaching them that they are worthy of self-love and self-care. And this knowledge will make all the difference.

For many of us, the idea of giving our daughters gifts we have yet to fully receive or embrace in our own lives (i.e. self-love, self-care, self-acceptance, and self-worth) can feel scary. Please know, dear woman, that this is the beauty of the Heroines Club *Mother*-Daughter Empowerment Circle: as we bless our daughters, we heal ourselves. By raising our daughters to know they are worthy, we begin to understand more about our own worth.

We are in this together.

Love,
Melia

Getting to Know Our Heroine

Malala Yousafzai (born July 12, 1997) is a Pakistani activist who, while a teenager, spoke out publicly about the Taliban's prohibition on the education of girls. She gained global attention when she survived an assassination attempt at age fifteen. She is also the youngest Nobel Prize winner in history.

Malala was born in a dangerous region of the world called the Swat Valley in Mingora, Pakistan. She was born into a loving Sunni Muslim family and has two younger brothers. Her mother is a homemaker and her father is a poet, school owner, and educational activist himself, running a chain of private schools for boys and girls. As a young girl, Malala went to school at one of her father's schools. She was a bright student and loved learning. After school each day, Malala was a typical young girl: she played with her friends outside, watched television, and often fought with her little brothers. Life was pleasant for Malala and her family until 2007, when everything changed. A violent group of fighters called the Taliban invaded and took over the city where she lived. Taliban members follow an extreme view of the peaceful religion of Islam, and they believe that women and girls are not worthy of any freedoms, including an education.

Life under the Taliban regime was terrible. Televisions, computers, DVDs, music, video games, and non-religious books were all banned. Girls and women were forced to stay home, unless accompanied by a male relative. Adult women could no longer go to the market alone. Nor could they hold jobs, vote, or even go to the doctor or the hospital. All girls' schools had to close immediately, or be destroyed. Anyone caught disobeying the Taliban was severely punished.

Malala was afraid, but most of all, she was outraged that the Taliban had taken away her right to an education. She had dreamed of becoming a doctor, or maybe a politician, and knew that her education was important and required for her dreams to come true. In 2008, Malala spoke at a local press conference about education rights, in a speech called "How Dare the Taliban Take Away My Basic Right to Education?" Newspapers and television covered her speech. Later that year, she began writing a blog for the British Broadcasting Company detailing her life under Taliban occupation, their attempts to take control of the valley, and her views on promoting education for girls. Shortly after, *The New York Times* made a documentary about her life, featuring Malala and her father.

In 2009, the war between the Taliban and the Pakistan army ended, and the Taliban retreated into the hills. Malala's school reopened and life went back to how it had been before. Malala continued to rise in prominence and was nominated for the International Children's Peace Prize. In 2011, Malala was awarded Pakistan's National Youth Peace Prize. Malala had become famous for her advocacy, and the Taliban now knew who she was. They issued many frightening death threats against her, but Malala and her family did not initially believe that anyone would actually hurt a child. They were wrong.

On October 9, 2012, the Taliban tried to assassinate fifteen-year-old Malala Yousafzai. A gunman boarded the truck she and her classmates used as a school bus and asked the question, "Who is Malala?" Once her identity was revealed, the gunman shot her in the head. The shooting had left her in critical condition, so she was flown to a military hospital in Peshwar, and then transferred to Birmingham, England. Although she required multiple surgeries, Malala survived and suffered no major brain damage. Malala showed courage and optimism during her long recovery, and continued to speak out on the importance of education. Following this tragic event, there was a world-wide outpouring of support and an international movement was born.

On her sixteenth birthday, Malala gave a speech to the United Nations. She has since written an autobiography, *I Am Malala: The Girl Who Stood Up for Education and Was Shot by the Taliban.* In 2014, Malala was awarded the prestigious Nobel Peace Prize for her activism. With the prize earnings, she started the Malala Fund to help children all over the world receive an education. On her eighteenth birthday, Malala opened a school in the Bekaa Valley, Lebanon, for Syrian refugees.

Malala has become an international symbol for peace and she inspires girls and women today to know that they are worthy of their rights, and to stand up for them.

Discussion Prompts

1.   Malala became an activist when she was very young. Where do you think she found the inspiration and courage?

2.   Malala had a very unique and close relationship with her father. Who has been a mentor in your life, and how did they inspire you?

3.   Discuss Malala's relationship with her mother. How did Malala's mother influence her? How do you think Malala's mother felt about her daughter's activism?

4.   How is Malala, her life and her story, similar to the heroine Anne Frank?

5.   Malala and her family now live in Birmingham, England. Have you ever been uprooted in your life? What helped you adapt?

6.   What role does education play in your life? How has getting to know Malala this month affected your personal experience of education or impacted the value you place on learning?

7. Why do you think education is considered a basic human right? What other basic human rights do you believe people are entitled to?

8. What does self-worth mean to you? How do you experience self-worth?

9. Do you think you have to "prove yourself" in some way to be worthy?

Do you have to be great at something?

Do you have to be incredibly popular or part of the "in" crowd?

Do you have to be exceptionally good-looking?

Is there any reason why someone should not be entitled to a good sense of self-worth?

10. Where do you think high self-worth comes from? What might cause low self-worth?

11. How does one's sense of self-worth impact how they care for themselves?

12. What does this month's affirmation, "I Am Worthy" mean to you?

Integrated Activities

The Red Thread of Worth

To symbolize our inherent worth as human beings, and our connection with our sisters all around the world, we will participate in an ancient women's circle ritual called 'The Red Thread.'

SUPPLIES

◎ Ball of red yarn or string

◎ Scissors

INSTRUCTIONS

The facilitator begins by holding the end of the yarn in her left hand and wrapping the yarn around her left wrist twice—once for herself and once for women and girls everywhere. As she wraps the yarn, she will speak the words "I am worthy of ___." She will then pass the ball of yarn to the circle sister on her left, who will then wrap the yarn twice—once for herself and once for her sisters everywhere—while speaking the words, "I am worthy of ___," and so on all the way around the circle. Once the ball of yarn has made its way around the circle, the facilitator will speak about the symbolism of the red string (to remind us of our inherent worth and to send that powerful energetic medicine out to our sisters all around the world.) Carefully pass the scissors around the circle, allowing each member a turn to cut her string from the web and tie the ends together, making a bracelet. This bracelet will serve as a potent reminder of our inherent, unconditional worth.

Book Swap

Malala once said, "Extremists have shown what frightens them most: a girl with a book." This integrated activity honors Malala's message and celebrates the gift of books. Also, book swaps are a fun way to turn a stack of old books into a whole new set of exciting reads you and your daughter will enjoy!

SUPPLIES

◎ Books—Invite mothers and daughters to bring as many of their old books as they would like!

◎ Space—Make sure you have plenty of space to display all the books. You may wish to have a long table or shelves available.

INSTRUCTIONS

Invite the circle to share a little bit about the books they brought, talking about why the books have been special to them. Depending on the size and dynamics of your circle, the exchange can be a free-for-all, or you can control it by having mother-daughter pairs choose a number (mother-daughter pair number one chooses first, and so on.) After the swap is complete and everyone has had a turn, offer time for sharing about the books that were chosen and why they were drawn to them. Any leftover books can be donated to the local library, charity shop or a women's center in Malala's honor.

Medicine Meditation

Set your things to the side, find a comfortable, fully-supported resting position, perhaps take your mother's hand if that would feel good to you, and begin to follow your breath. In your mind's eye, let's travel together to Birmingham, England, to the home of Malala and her family. Her mother and father welcome you at the door, and point you in the direction of Malala's room. As you step into the partially opened bedroom door, you see Malala sitting comfortably on her bed reading a book. When she sees you, she smiles, closes her book, and invites you in. In your mind's eye, sit down next to Malala on the bed and introduce yourself. Thank her for her courage and strength in advocating for the worthiness of girls everywhere. Is there anything you would like to ask Malala or share with her about your own life? You may do that now. Listen for her response. As you look at Malala here in this moment, what words come to mind? What words or phrases describe the medicine of Malala Yousafzai to you? When you are ready, send Malala your love and gratitude, give her a hug if you like, and gently open your eyes and return to our circle.

Quote Study

"Honor your daughters. They are honorable."

"For my brothers it was easy to think about the future. They can be anything they want. But for me it was hard and for that reason I wanted to become educated and empower myself with knowledge."

"In some parts of the world, students are going to school every day. It's their normal life. But in other parts of the world, we are starving for education . . . it's like a precious gift. It's like a diamond."

"I am stronger than fear."

"The best way to solve problems and to fight against war is through dialogue."

"Let us remember: one book, one pen, one child, and one teacher can change the world."

"When the whole world is silent, even one voice becomes powerful."

"We call upon our sisters around the world to be brave—to embrace the strength within themselves and realize their full potential."

Recommended Resources

Books for Mothers and Daughters, ages 7+

Malala Yousafzai: Warrior with Words, by Abouraya, K.

Who is Malala Yousafzai? by Brown, D.

Books for Mothers and Daughters, ages 10+

I am Malala: How One Girl Stood Up for Education and Changed the World (Young Readers Edition), by Malala Yousafzai

Books for Mothers and Daughters, ages 12+

I am Malala: The Girl Who Stood Up for Education and Was Shot by the Taliban, by Malala Yousafzai

Film

He Named Me Malala (2015)

Music

"I Am Malala" (2013) by Girls of the World

Web

www.youtube.com/malalayousafzai

www.malala.org

ADDITIONAL RECOMMENDED RESOURCES FOR MOTHERS

The Confident Child: Raising Children to Believe in Themselves, by Apter, T.

The Gifts of Imperfection: Let Go of Who You Think You're Supposed to Be and Embrace Who You Are, by Brown, B.

I Thought It Was Just Me (but it isn't): Making the Journey from "What Will People Think?" to "I Am Enough", by Brown, B.

ROSALIND FRANKLIN

"I Am My Mother's Daughter"

Dear Mothers,

As covered in-depth in the second chapter, *The Power of Conscious Storytelling,* our daughters benefit tremendously from knowing the stories of whom and where they come from. This month, inspired by our heroine's phenomenal exploration of DNA, we will explicitly connect our daughters to the great web of kin and legacy to which they belong.

Our DNA contains a record of our ancestors. We carry their genetic signature in our bodies, our features, and even our traits. At fertilization, we receive 50% of our nuclear DNA from each of our parents, who received 50% of theirs from each of their parents, and so on. This nuclear DNA acts like a recipe holding the instructions telling our bodies how to develop and function. In addition to nuclear DNA, each fertilized egg also contains an exact copy of the mother's mitochondrial DNA, but none of the father's. The result is that mitochondrial DNA is passed on only along the maternal line. This means that all of the mitochondrial DNA in the cells of a person's body are exact copies of her mothers', and all of the mother's mitochondrial DNA is an exact copy of her mother's and so on. All women from the same maternal lineage carry the same

If you want to understand any woman, you must first ask about her mother and then listen carefully.

Anita Diamant,
The Red Tent

exact mitochondrial DNA. It's fascinating, really!

Dr. Naomi Lowinsky gave a name to the generations of women who carry within them the history and biology of a family: she called it the **Motherline**. This month, we will honor our Motherlines as living threads in the tapestries of who we are.

Finding our female roots, reclaiming our feminine souls, requires paying attention to our mothers' lives and experience; listening to our mothers' stories, and our grandmothers' stories, is the beginning of understanding our own. When we hear these stories, we tap into the wisdom of our Motherline.

Dr. Naomi Lowinsky

This month at home

The roots from which we grow are planted in the fertile ground of our ancestors. A good way to find out more about who you are, and to know yourself better, is to learn about the ancestors who produced you.

In regard to your Motherline, I encourage you and your daughter to:

Learn their names

The names of the women from which we come are medicine to our souls. Most of us know the names of our grandmothers, but what about *their* mothers, and *their* mothers, and *their* mothers? This month, research your matrilineal heritage, and collect as many names as you can. These precious names will be shared in an integrated activity this month.

Hear their stories

Honor the grandmothers, the mother of mothers. If you are blessed enough to still be able to communicate with them on the physical plane, I encourage you to make it happen. Every time you speak to one of the elders in your family, you are almost always guaranteed to learn more about the people who came before you. Give yourself and your daughter this gift of legacy. If the grandmothers in your lineage are no longer alive, speak with aunts and great-aunts. If you are unable to meet and speak with the women from whom you come, consider inviting them into your dreamtime, or channeling them through intuitive painting or journaling.

It may be helpful to spend some time contemplating, or even researching if necessary, your matrilineal heritage and make a list of the stories you want your daughter to know and why. Excavate stories of strength, courage, compassion, and wisdom, and offer them to your daughter.

See their faces

A photograph of an ancestor can really bring your Motherline to life—a reminder that this was a baby/girl/woman who really lived! If you don't have many (or any) photos of your foremothers, take the opportunity this month to ask family members for any they may have. Today it is easy to make copies—you can take a digital photograph of the photo, or photographs can be scanned with a scanner. Bring the photographs to circle with you this month for one of the integrated activities.

Make the connections

Connect your daughter to her place in your Motherline circuitry by telling her about all the endearing ways in which she may be like her foremothers. What features or traits do you see in her that remind you of the women from your Motherline? Every day presents opportunities to highlight your daughter's connection to her ancestors. Making these connections does not have to be scheduled and planned; it can occur in little bursts throughout the normal unfolding of the day.

When your daughter is sick and you are caring for her, tell her about how your mother cared for you when you were little and sick. Does she enjoy playing the piano, just like her great-grandmother, or does her unbounded laugh remind you of her auntie's? *Tell her.* These seemingly random tidbits will not only strengthen the bond between you, they will also create a deep sense of belonging in your daughter.

Our female souls are rooted in our matrilineal legacy, and there is an ancient female wisdom that lives in the depths of stories from that line. By exploring our Motherlines with our daughters this month, we will transform our potent mother-daughter dyads into even deeper, ancient, sacred female connections.

We are in this together.

Love,
Melia

Getting to Know Our Heroine

Rosalind Elsie Franklin (1920–1958) was a scientist of the highest caliber, best known for her role in the one of the greatest scientific discoveries of all time: the structure of DNA.

Rosalind was born into an affluent and influential family in London, England. As a girl, she displayed exceptional intelligence, with a strong passion for science. She received an excellent education from St. Paul's Girls' School, one of the few institutions at the time that taught physics and chemistry to girls. By age fifteen, Rosalind knew she wanted to devote her life to science. Rosalind's father, however, actively discouraged her interest in science and wanted her to focus her education, talent, and skills on more charitable forms of community service. When Rosalind graduated, she wanted to attend university, but her father, who was decidedly against higher education for women, refused to pay. Rosalind's mother was on her daughter's side, and an aunt stepped in, agreeing to pay. Rosalind overcame her father's opposition, and attended Cambridge University, majoring in physical chemistry.

World War II was going on at the time, and so when Rosalind graduated college, she had to decide whether to be drafted for more traditional war work or pursue a PhD-oriented research job in a field relevant to wartime needs. She chose the latter, and began work studying coal. Her coal work was used in the development of gas masks, a valuable contribution to England under attack. Her work yielded a doctoral thesis and Rosalind received her PhD from Cambridge in 1945.

After the war, Rosalind was awarded a fellowship at King's College in London to use her superior scientific techniques to investigate DNA. The climate for women at King's College was oppressive and discriminatory. For example, only males were allowed in the university dining rooms, and after hours, Rosalind's colleagues went to men-only pubs. Within this "boys' club" culture at the university, Rosalind performed her precise and detailed work essentially in isolation.

Rosalind worked very hard and took increasingly clear X-ray diffraction photos of DNA. She quickly discovered there were two forms of DNA—wet and dry—and that both forms had two helices. This quiet discovery, made alone by Rosalind in the basement lab of King's College, was a world-shaking achievement. However, because she was a woman in a male-dominated institution, male scientists took credit for her research and findings. Maurice Wilkins, a chauvinistic scientist where Rosalind worked, secretly removed photos from Rosalind's records without her knowledge or permission, and showed them to scientists Francis Crick and James

Watson. From Rosalind's photos, they gleaned crucial insights about DNA's structure, and the solution they had struggled to find became instantly clear. It was Rosalind who provided the painstakingly accumulated data they used to create their model, but Watson and Crick never told Rosalind they had seen her materials, nor did they directly acknowledge their debt to her work when they published their announcement of the DNA discovery. Rosalind never knew they had stolen her work.

When Rosalind learned that Watson and Crick had discovered the structure of DNA, she was no doubt disappointed because she herself was very close to discovering the structure, but ever the dedicated scientist, she moved forward and decided to transfer her fellowship to another institution to begin studying plant viruses. Her virus work laid the foundation of modern virology.

In the fall of 1956, at thirty-six years old, Rosalind was diagnosed with ovarian cancer, must likely caused by the frequent exposure to X-rays in her lab. For the next eighteen months, she underwent surgeries and other treatments, all the while continuing to work. Rosalind died of ovarian cancer in 1958.

In 1962, four years after Rosalind's death, Crick, Watson, and Wilkins were awarded the Nobel Prize in medicine for their work in solving the structure of DNA, and none gave Rosalind credit for her contributions. Fortunately, thanks to the work of historians and archivists, Rosalind's important contribution became widely known in the 1990s. Unfortunately, the Nobel Prize committee does not offer awards after a person's death.

Rosalind Franklin's scientific achievements in coal chemistry and virus structure research were considerable. Her peers in those fields acknowledged this during her life and after her death. But it is her role in the discovery of DNA structure that has garnered the most public attention over the last decade. Rosalind, cheated of a Nobel Prize by misogynistic colleagues, is the unsung heroine behind the discovery of DNA's double helix. During a time when women's achievements were downplayed and undermined, Rosalind persevered and accomplished important work in her field. Today there are many facilities, scholarships, and research grants, especially those for women, named in her honor.

Discussion Prompts

1. The other (all male) scientists at King's College referred to Rosalind behind her back as "Rosy," which is an adjective meaning 'encouraging' or 'upbeat'. This demeaning nickname was said sarcastically, because they viewed Rosalind as difficult to work with as she was so outspoken, passionate, driven, and focused. Do you think if Rosalind would have been a man, those personality characteristics would have been viewed in the same way, or even noticed?

2. Have you ever been called a demeaning nickname? How did you handle it?

3. Franklin family vacations were often walking and hiking tours, and hiking became one of Rosalind's lifelong passions. Have you ever been hiking? Why do you think Rosalind enjoyed it so much?

4. Rosalind had a talent for languages. She spoke not only English, but also French, Italian, and German! Have you studied another language? Which languages might you be interested in learning?

5. Rosalind's mother once said, "All her life, Rosalind knew exactly where she was going, and at sixteen, she took science for her subject." Mothers, what were your career interests at sixteen years old? How have they changed or remained the same over the years?

Daughters, which academic areas do you wish to "take for your subject?" What do you most enjoy learning about?

6.   Have you ever experienced someone taking credit for your work or efforts? How did you handle it?

7.   Do you think women in science still face obstacles in science today? Do you think that women scientists are still discriminated against the way Rosalind was in the 1950s?

8.   Rosalind studied DNA. DNA is the material that carries all the information about how a living thing will look and function. DNA determines hereditary characteristics, such as eye color and personality behavior. What do you imagine has been passed on through your DNA?

9.   At the moment of your miraculous conception, your genetic makeup was set. Your hairline, the soft freckles on your face, the size and shape of your hips, the curve of your neck—all of this and so much more—was predetermined, and for good reason. Our bodies are built to survive and thrive. Your ancestors needed their unique body structure to complete the tasks of their time, and now, many generations later, you bear the proof. How has researching your ancestors affected your body image? How might you honor your ancestors through your relationship with your body?

10. What does this month's affirmation, "I Am My Mother's Daughter," mean to you?

Integrated Activities

"And the Winner is, Rosalind Franklin!"

Each recipient of a Nobel Prize receives a gold medal, a diploma, and a large sum of money. Although the Nobel Prize Committee does not offer awards post-humously, the Heroines Club does! For this integrated activity, we will make Nobel Prize medals for Rosalind Franklin.

SUPPLIES

◎ Yellow construction paper, cut into the circular shape of a medal. Enough for each mother-daughter pair to have one.

◎ Items and supplies to decorate the "medal," such as markers, stickers, stencils, glitter, etc.

INSTRUCTIONS

Each mother-daughter pair will make a Nobel Prize medal to honor the contributions of Rosalind Franklin. Write words and/or draw pictures and symbols to personalize the medal for Rosalind. After the allotted time, gather supplies and clean the area. Allow time for each mother-daughter pair to share the medal they created. After sharing with the circle, place the medals on the central altar near the photograph of Rosalind. The facilitator will close this integrated activity by leading the circle in speaking these words together: "We see you, we hear you, our sister Rosalind. Thank you for your supreme scientific contributions."

Calling in the Motherline

"I am Melia, daughter of Sandra, daughter of Angelina Else, daughter of Maria, daughter of Anna, mother of Della Ruth. "

"I am Della Ruth, daughter of Melia, daughter of Sandra, daughter of Angelina Else, daughter of Maria, daughter of Anna."

So starts one of my favorite ceremonial activities!

INSTRUCTIONS

Moving around the circle, each circle member will call in her Motherline by speaking the names of the women from which she comes, beginning with her own name. Circle members are invited to share any photographs, relics, or meaningful heirlooms from their Motherline during this integrated activity.

Matryoshka Motherline Dolls

Amazing fact: the cell you came from was once inside your mother's fetus in her mother's womb!

Nesting dolls are probably one of the oldest toys. They represent generations of women in the family and date back to the times when families were matrilineal.

SUPPLIES

◎ One set of blank, unpainted matryoshka nesting dolls per mother-daughter pair. These wooden craft dolls can be purchased at most craft stores or online.

◎ Paint pens and markers

Like those old pear-shaped Russian dolls that open at the middle to reveal another and another, down to the pea-sized, irreducible minimum, may we carry our mothers forth in our bellies. May we, borne onward by our daughters, ride the Envelope of Almost-Infinity, that chain letter good for the next twenty-five thousand days of their lives.

Maxine Kumin

These dolls will represent your unique Motherline. Begin by writing the names of all the women your daughter comes from, in order, with her as the largest doll, containing all of her matrilineal ancestors. So, for example, my daughter Della would be the largest doll, opening to a doll with my name, opening to a doll with her grandmother's (my mother's) name, opening to a doll with her great-grandmother's name, and so on depending on the number of dolls in your set. After the names have been written, spend time together decorating the dolls with paint pens and markers, personalizing them with faces, hair, and clothing. After the allotted time is complete, collect supplies and clean the area. Allow time for mothers and daughters to share their creations with the circle.

Medicine Meditation

Set your things to the side, find a comfortable, fully-supported resting position, perhaps take your mother's hand if that would feel good to you, and begin to follow your breath. In your mind's eye, let's travel together to Rosalind's lab in the basement of King's College in London. Rosalind is there working. She is grateful to have your company and she wants to show you all of her instruments and how they work. Rosalind moves with an excited energy as she shows you her most recent photographs she has captured of DNA. She is so very proud of her work! Do you have a question for Rosalind, or something you would like to share with her? Speak from your heart and listen to her response. What message does Rosalind have for you about science, about life, about being a woman, or about the beautiful evidence of the Motherline she sees reflected in her photographs of DNA? Receive her words and thank her for her wisdom. As you look at Rosalind here in this moment, what words come to mind? What words or phrases describe the medicine of Rosalind Franklin to you? When you are ready, send her your love and gratitude, and gently open your eyes and return to our circle.

Quote Study

"Science and everyday life cannot and should not be separated."

"In my view, all that is necessary for faith is the belief that by doing our best we shall succeed in our aims: the improvement of humankind."

"Science, for me, gives a partial explanation for life. In so far as it goes, it is based on fact, experience, and experiment."

"What's the use of doing all this work if we don't get some fun out of this?"

Recommended Resources

BOOKS FOR MOTHERS AND DAUGHTERS AGES 7+

Rosalind Franklin (Scientists Who Made History), by Senker, C.

Rosalind Franklin's Beautiful Twist, by Friedman, M.

BOOKS FOR MOTHERS AND DAUGHTERS AGE 12+

Rosalind Franklin: The Dark Lady of DNA, by Maddox, B.

Rosalind Franklin and DNA, by Sayre, A.

FILM

DNA – Secret of Photo 51 (2003)

Rosalind Franklin: DNA's Dark Lady (2003)

WEB

www.biography.com/people/rosalind-franklin-9301344

http://jwa.org/encyclopedia/article/franklin-rosalind

ADDITIONAL RECOMMENDED TITLES FOR MOTHERS

The Motherline: Every Woman's Journey to Find Her Female Roots, by Lowinsky, N.

Mother-Daughter Wisdom: Understanding the Crucial Link Between Mothers, Daughters, and Health, by Northrup, C.

MAYA ANGELOU

"I Speak My Truth"

Dear Mothers,

In 2013, Dr. Maya Angelou was the keynote speaker at a speech-language-hearing convention in Atlanta, Georgia. I will always remember the way the room instantly became electrified the moment she entered. Every audience member jumped to their feet and applauded with great fervor for over five minutes, as Maya, seated in a wheelchair and wearing shades over her eyes, smiled with utmost dignity. At eighty-five years old, Maya commanded the total attention of the entire auditorium, packed to the ceiling, and she had not yet even spoken a word! I was overcome with emotion and tears began streaming down my face. I always loved Maya's work and her story, but in that moment, I saw her for the truly powerful woman she was. Maya Angelou had spent her life speaking her truth, and the world loved her for it.

Only one thing is more frightening than speaking your truth. And that is not speaking.

Naomi Wolf

What does it mean to "speak your truth"?

Actors spend hours rehearsing, learning lines, developing accents and gestures, and considering motivations as they embody a character. After a performance, actors shed these "masks" and return to themselves. In some aspects of our lives, we may perform as if we are actors, hiding behind an image and speaking the lines we think we are supposed to say. When we do this, we are not being authentic or true to ourselves. Our Highest Self calls us to release any words that are not in alignment with our true nature, and instead, speak our truth.

Speaking your truth is an essential aspect of living a life of passion, fulfillment, authenticity, in true connection with others. In her 2008 book, *Letter to My Daughter*, Maya Angelou writes, "I wish we could stop the little lies. I don't mean that one has to be brutally frank. I don't believe we should be brutal about anything; however, it is wonderfully liberating to be honest. One does not have to tell all that one knows, but we should be careful what we do say is the truth."

Speaking your truth means:

◎ Taking off any "masks" you wear.

◎ Refusing to be anyone you are not.

◎ Not worrying about what others may think.

◎ Participating earnestly and in good faith during tough conversations.

◎ Voicing your thoughts, feelings, beliefs, values, and opinions.

It does not mean:

◎ Ensuring everyone knows your opinion on every issue.

◎ Judging others.

◎ Giving unsolicited advice.

◎ Giving others a "piece of your mind."

◎ Getting up on a "soap box."

◎ Getting in people's faces and challenging them.

◎ Your truth is *the* truth. There is no truth with a capital T in the human condition; there is only "my" truth, "your" truth, "her" truth, "his" truth, and "their" truth.

Interestingly, speaking your truth is actually more defined by your relationship with yourself than it is by other people. It is a moment-to-moment decision to express how you truly feel and what is real for you in an authentic, transparent, and kind way. It is keeping both your words and your actions in alignment with that which is in your heart.

We practice speaking our truths together in circle every month. When the talking stick makes its way into your hands, before you speak, you are encouraged to pause, drop to your center, have a breath, and notice what truths are living inside of you.

What if I don't know what my truth is?

Speaking your truth requires awareness and a willingness to take an honest look at yourself. Ask yourself: *What is my truth here on this issue? What do I really feel inside?*

Your body will let you know when you have a truth to tell. You may experience a burning conviction that *this must be said and it must be said by me.* You may feel surges of power in your gut, heart, or throat. You may feel a quickening in your chest, or a rising of energy in your mouth. When you don't speak your truth, or when you avoid the truth, if often feels like betraying yourself.

I have found that free-writing/journaling offers a direct path to personal truth. When you find yourself feeling confused about your soul's truth, set a timer for five minutes, and begin with the simple writing prompt, "What I really want to say is . . . " Like peeling the outer layers of an onion, this writing prompt will take you to the core of your truth.

What if I'm afraid?

Acting with courage and choosing to speak your truth when the stakes are high will be an incredible source of pride. The more uncomfortable conversations are frequently the ones that move us closer to what we really want, and often the hardest truths are also the most valuable.

Speaking truth is like a muscle we build with practice, and it can feel scary at first. Our culture often prioritizes politeness over clear and direct communication, and saying what we *really* think can be considered rude or offensive. Many of us grew up hearing the dictum, "If you can't say anything nice, don't say anything at all." Because of this, we have learned to keep our thoughts and feelings to ourselves because of worry that people will not love us if they hear our raw, authentic truth. We silence ourselves because we are afraid of possible rejection, offending others, appearing pessimistic, losing someone's approval, or breaking a relationship's connection.

According to Susan Campbell, PhD, author of *Saying What's Real: Seven Keys to Authentic Communication and Relationship Success,* it is possible to enjoy both connection and integrity. The key is in finding ways to clearly voice our perspectives, while also expressing care and respect for those willing to hear us. Speaking your truth can be done with grace, tact, and respect. As I often tell my children, "Say what you mean, but don't say it mean." When your truth is difficult for others to accept, you may make it easier to accept in how you say it, but it does not mean you must not say it. It is true that either the relationship will dissolve in response to your truth, or the connection you share will deepen and become even stronger, but **it is not within your control, nor your responsibility, for how your truth affects others.**

Guiding our daughters to speak their truth

The message girls receive in our culture is to be passive and "nice." They are taught that it is preferable to keep the peace rather than to speak up with an opinion that might be unpopular. Counteracting this message and teaching our daughters to speak their truth will keep them safer and more fulfilled.

A girl who is not living and speaking her truth will often:

◎ Have trouble saying "no" to friends.

◎ Have trouble standing up to teasers when in a bystander role.

◎ Not try things she is interested in, or stop doing the things she is interested in, if they are not deemed "cool" by her peers.

◎ "Dumb herself down" and present herself as less intelligent than she is.

◎ Change her mind based on whom she is interacting with.

◎ Value the opinions and wants of her peers more than her own.

As you can imagine, a girl who does not feel confident in speaking her truth is at risk for frequent hardships and pain. For her safety and well-being, we must guide our daughters to express their values, beliefs, needs, and desires with courage and compassion. We must guide them to listen for their deep inner "yes" and their deep inner "no," and to have the confidence to convey both with clarity and grace.

A final thought on speaking truth

Above all else, our daughters need to know that they can come to us, their mothers, and tell us the truth—no matter what. At some point this month, and then again many times throughout her life, explicitly tell your daughter: "I will always be available to listen, to support, and to believe. There is nothing you can do, or not do, that will shock me, disappoint me, or make me stop loving you as much as I did in the first moment I looked into your newly born eyes. *No matter what,* you can come to me if you are ever curious, confused, or in trouble. You don't ever have to hide your truth from me."

We are in this together.

Love,
Melia

Getting to Know Our Heroine

Marguerite Annie "Maya" Johnson Angelou (1928–2014), one of the most renowned and influential voices of our time, was a celebrated poet, memoirist, educator, dancer, dramatist, producer, actress, historian, filmmaker, and civil rights activist. She is perhaps most well-known for her 1969 acclaimed memoir, *I Know Why the Caged Bird Sings*, which made history as the first non-fiction best-seller by an African-American woman. With elegance, honesty, and detail, Maya wrote about her life experiences as a young African-American girl growing up in the segregated American South, creating a poignant account of the social and political climate of the 1930s and offering a record of American history for generations to come.

Like many of our heroines, Maya had a difficult childhood. At three years old, Maya's parents divorced and she and her four-year-old brother, Bailey, were sent alone by train to live with their father's mother in the rural southern town of Stamps, Arkansas. In the segregated South, Maya experienced firsthand racial prejudices and discrimination.

A terrible thing happened to Maya when she was eight years old. On a visit back to her mother, Maya was sexually abused by her mother's man friend. At first, Maya told no one, but her mother and brother noticed how upset she was and she told them her truth. The man was charged in court and found guilty, but he was only jailed for one day. After he was released, he was beaten to death, most likely by Maya's uncles. Maya was so deeply traumatized by what happened, and by the power of her words to "kill a man," that she completely stopped speaking for five years. It was during this period of silence that Maya developed her extraordinary memory, her love for books and literature, and her ability to listen and observe the world around her. During that time, Maya's grandma was patient with her granddaughter's silence, often telling her that she knew Maya was wise, and that she would speak when she was ready. Eventually, at age thirteen, Maya did begin to speak again.

When Maya was a teenager, her love for the arts and her strong academic skills won her a scholarship to study dance and drama in California, at San Francisco's Labor School. A few weeks after graduation, Maya gave birth to her only child—a son she named Clyde. Maya took on the difficult life of a single mother, supporting herself and her son by working day jobs as a waitress and cook, but she had not given up on her talents for music, dance, performance, and poetry.

In the 1950s, her career in theater took off; she participated in touring productions internationally, as well as off-Broadway productions. In 1961, Maya lived abroad in Egypt, and then in Ghana, working as an educator, editor, and freelance writer. During her time abroad, Maya studied and mastered six languages in addition to English. Upon returning to the United States, Maya wrote about her life experiences and spoke her truth in her first memoir, *I Know Why the Caged Bird Sings,* making her an international star. Maya went on to write six more autobiographies, three books of essays, several books of poetry, and many plays, movies, and television shows.

Maya was close friends with many other truth-telling heroines and heroes in her lifetime, such as Malcolm X, James Baldwin, Martin Luther King, Coretta Scott King, Billie Holiday, and Oprah Winfrey. She received many prestigious awards for her work and she taught at several American universities. Although Maya never attended college, she received over fifty honorary doctorate degrees. In 2011, Maya was presented the highest civilian award for service, the Presidential Medal of Freedom.

By speaking and living her truth, Maya kicked the door of truth-telling wide open for the rest of us. Maya Angelou continues to inspire girls and women today to find their voices, and use them to speak their truth—loud and clear.

Discussion Prompts

1. Maya wrote seven autobiographies in her lifetime, the first of which she titled *I Know Why the Caged Bird Sings*. Why do you think she chose that title? If you were to write a memoir of your life, what might be a fitting title?

2. As a girl, Maya loved to read. On her list of favorite authors were William Shakespeare, Edgar Allan Poe, and Langston Hughes. Who are your favorite authors? What kind of books do you most enjoy reading?

3. Maya loved to cook. She even published two cookbooks! What's something that you love that you might want to write a book about?

4. Maya was named "Marguerite" as a baby, but her beloved brother called her "mya sister," which was eventually shortened to

"Maya." Does your family have a nickname for you? What is the story behind it?

5.   A terrible thing happened to Maya when she was eight years old. She was sexually abused by a man friend of her mother's. One day, while they were in the house alone, the man touched Maya on her private body parts—her labia, vagina, and bottom. At first Maya didn't tell anyone, because even though sexual abuse is *never* the child's fault, she felt scared and ashamed. Finally, Maya told her mother and brother, and they helped her by listening and talking to her. If something ever happened to you that made you feel scared or ashamed, it is important that you tell an adult you trust. Who are some adults that you trust and could talk to about anything?

6.   How does your body feel when you are speaking your truth as compared to when you are remaining silent or avoiding the truth?

7.   Have you ever been pressured by a friend to do something you didn't want to do? How did you handle it?

8.   Do you find it more difficult to speak your truth to friends, or to people you don't know very well? Why might that be?

9.   Have you ever heard of the metaphor "the elephant in the room?" This metaphor represents times when an obvious truth is either being ignored or left unaddressed. When I hear this metaphor, I always imagine two people sitting on couches across from one another with a large elephant between them! How does not addressing the "elephant in the room" damage relationships and create walls or barriers between people?

10.   What does this month's affirmation, "I Speak My Truth," mean to you?

Integrated Activities

This Little Light of Mine

Maya once said, "Nothing can dim the light which shines from within." Inspired by these wise words, this integrated activity symbolizes our own inner light and truth.

SUPPLIES

◎ White, plain, glass jar candles. Enough for every circle member to have her own.

◎ Sharpie markers (or other permanent glass markers) in an assortment of colors.

◎ Stickers, adhesive gems, ribbon, and other decorating craft supplies.

INSTRUCTIONS

Take a few deep breaths, calming and opening your heart and mind to the creative journey about to unfold. You may choose to play soft, meditative music in the background, while encouraging mothers and daughters to share the experience by working alongside one another and conversing quietly. Using the provided craft supplies, decorate the outside of your glass jar to represent your inner light and truth. You may wish to write your name and this month's affirmation, "I Speak My Truth," on your jar as well. Have fun with this and let your intuition be your guide!

Once the allotted time is complete, clean the area and gather supplies. Allow time for mothers and daughters to share their creations with the circle. Each circle member now has a personalized candle to take home as a reminder to be guided by the light of truth. Encourage mothers and daughters to place them in a safe location and enjoy lighting them together during special mother-daughter times.

Maya Dance Party

Maya loved to sing and dance! She even recorded two albums: *Miss Calypso* in 2003, and *Caged Bird Songs* in 2014. Choose one of Maya's songs and have a mother-daughter dance party! As Maya's deep, rich voice fills the room, feel your heart opening wide while your body flows with the music.

Medicine Meditation

Set your things to the side, find a comfortable, fully-supported resting position, perhaps take your mother's hand if that would feel good to you, and begin to follow your breath. In your mind's eye, travel with me to Maya Angelou's home. She is seated on a comfortable couch in her living room, and she is expecting you. Join Maya on the couch and let her take your hands in hers. Look into her eyes and feel the warmth of her smile. What would you like to ask Maya today? Is there something that you've been keeping to yourself that you need to express, but don't know how? Ask Maya. You may ask her anything you wish. Listen to her response and offer her gratitude for her wisdom. As you look into Maya's eyes in this moment, what word or phrase comes to mind? That word or phrase is the part of the medicine that Maya offers us. Take a few more breaths, send your love to Maya, and when you are ready, open your eyes.

Quote Study

"There is no greater agony than bearing an untold story inside you."

"I've learned that people will forget what you said, people will forget what you did, but people will never forget how you made them feel."

"You are the sum total of everything you've ever seen, heard, eaten, smelled, been told, forgot—it's all there. Everything influences each of us, and because of that, I try to make sure that my experiences are positive."

"Courage is the most important of all virtues, because without courage, you can't practice any other virtue consistently."

"You don't have to tell everything you know, but try to make everything you say the truth as you understand it."

"You alone are enough. You have nothing to prove to anybody."

"My wish for you is that you continue. Continue to be who and how you are, to astonish a mean world with your acts of kindness."

Recommended Resources

BOOKS FOR MOTHERS AND DAUGHTERS, AGES 7+

Maya Angelou: Journey of the Heart, by Pettit, J.

Who Was Maya Angelou? by Labrecque, E.

Poetry for Young People: Maya Angelou, by Wilson, E.

Life Doesn't Frighten Me, by Maya Angelou

BOOKS FOR MOTHERS AND DAUGHTERS, AGES 12+

Maya Angelou: A Biography of an Award-Winning Poet and Civil Rights Activist, by Agins, D.

Maya Angelou: The Complete Poetry, by Maya Angelou

Rainbow in the Cloud: The Wisdom and Spirit of Maya Angelou, by Maya Angelou

Letter to My Daughter, by Maya Angelou

FILM FOR MOTHERS AND DAUGHTERS AGES 12+

I Know Why the Caged Bird Sings (1999)

MUSIC

"Caged Bird Songs" by Maya Angelou (2014)

"Miss Calypso" by Maya Angelou (2003)

WEB

Maya Angelou YouTube Channel
http://www.mayaangelou.com/

ADDITIONAL RECOMMENDED RESOURCES FOR MOTHERS

I Know Why the Caged Bird Sings, by Maya Angelou

Carry On, Warrior: The Power of Embracing Your Messy, Beautiful Life, by Doyle Melton, G.

Know Your Truth, Speak Your Truth, Live Your Truth, by Hannegan, E.

MOTHER TERESA

"I Am Changing the World"

Dear Mothers,

Part of any child's development of healthy self-esteem is making a habit of giving back to others. This month's beloved heroine, Mother Teresa, teaches our daughters that their lives matter and that who they are and what they do has an impact on the world, right now. This empowering message gives our daughters a sense of meaning for their lives and a confidence in their own inherent self-worth.

You change the world by being yourself.

Yoko Ono

Children often feel shocked, sad, or even scared when they begin to realize the dark sides of our world: hunger, poverty, homelessness, violence, racism, pollution, etc. Knowing that they can do something to make a difference fosters a sense of control that comforts them. Research shows that girls find a sense of power and purpose when they take action to support the people or causes they care about. Serving those in need helps our daughters learn firsthand that they have the ability to make a positive impact at any age. It also reassures them that if they were ever in need, help would be available.

This month, I invite you to consider ways that you might help your daughter channel her specific skills and passions to serve

Tell me, what is it you plan to do with your one wild and precious life?

Mary Oliver

the greater community. There are numerous ways that even our youngest heroines can volunteer and serve. As our beloved heroine teaches us this month, changing the world begins with love and compassion. What or who inspires passion or compassion in your daughter? Start there. For example, my daughter, Della, is a fervent animal lover. After brainstorming ideas together, Della decided to use her birthday as a way to inspire giving to animals in need. Rather than gifts, guests were asked to bring a small bag of dog food to donate to the local animal shelter. The day after the party, Della and I had so much *fun* delivering the nineteen bags of dog food to the grateful staff at the animal shelter!

Our goal this month is to ignite a passion in our daughters' hearts to go out and change the world, knowing, of course, that they already are . . . just by being in it.

We are in this together.

Love,
Melia

Getting to Know Our Heroine

Anjezë Gonxhe Bojaxhiu "Mother Teresa" (1910–1997), a Roman Catholic religious sister and missionary, was a world-renowned humanitarian who devoted her entire life to helping the poor, the sick, the needy, and the helpless. From the time she was a small girl in Yugoslavia, Mother Teresa had a heart for kindness and service. Her childhood home was often filled with those less fortunate, whom her mother and father welcomed with open arms for a meal, or perhaps even a place to spend the night. Her missionary work began when she was eighteen years old as a nun in Calcutta, India where she taught at a private school for girls for over fifteen years. During this time, she was moved by the presence of the sick and dying on the city's streets, just outside the high walls of her wealthy school. She felt a distinct call to leave the convent and serve in the streets of Calcutta.

At thirty-six years old and with what amounted to only two and a half cents, Mother Teresa walked out of the safe and comfortable convent and into the slums of India to live with and serve what she referred to as the "poorest of the poor." On her very first day, Mother Teresa started a school with five impoverished students who had never been formally educated before. Did this simple act of one courageous woman make a difference? It most certainly did, and that school still exists today! Soon, other nuns joined her and she formed the Missionaries of Charity, whose purpose was to offer care to people who were shunned and uncared for throughout society.

One of the first things the Missionaries of Charity did was to open a home for the dying. The local hospitals had no room or interest in caring for the dying—especially the dying poor—so the dying had no choice but to lie on the streets and suffer. When a dying person came or was brought to Mother Teresa and her sisters, they were met with care and concern. They were washed and given clean clothes, medicine, and, perhaps most important, someone to hold their hand, listen, stroke their foreheads, and comfort them with love in their last days. Mother Teresa and the Missionaries of Charity also opened orphanages and began working with people with leprosy and AIDS as well. Today, Mother Teresa's legacy expands globally, with homes established in hundreds of locations all over the world.

When we wonder if one person or one act of kindness can truly make a difference, we need only to think of the brave and inspiring life of Mother Teresa to know that the answer is, unequivocally: *Yes*.

Discussion Prompts

1.   We all change the world every day, just by being in it. Have you ever thought about what impact you want your life to have on the world? What would you like to be known and remembered for? What do you want to offer this world?

2.   There is an old saying, "Charity begins at home." What do you think this means?

3.   Mother Teresa once said that "Besides the poverty, material poverty . . . that makes the people die of hunger, die of cold, die in the streets—there is that great poverty of being unwanted, unloved, uncared for, having no one to call your own, having no one to smile . . . This is the great poverty." Do you think that there are different ways one might be poor, sick, needy, or helpless? Could someone with a lot of money still be "poor?" How can we show love and compassion to those that are suffering from what Mother Teresa called the "greatest poverty?"

4.   Compassion is the concern for the misfortune of another paired with the wish to help. What cause stirs compassion in you and how do you think you can help?

5.   Do you recall an experience in which you were shown compassion by another human being? How did that change your life? What did you learn?

6.   In what ways do you think your community might need your talents and gifts?

7.   If you could change anything in the world right now, what would it be?

8.   What does this month's affirmation, "I Am Changing the World," mean to you?

Integrated Activities

Love Notes

This month's integrated activity, inspired by our affirmation, is to practice kindness by creating surprise "love notes" to hide around your community. Because love spurs love, one of the most powerful ways that we change the world is by practicing random acts of kindness toward others. An encouraging love note can change someone's entire day and influence a dozen more acts of kindness!

SUPPLIES

◎ Index cards. Enough for everyone to have five.

◎ Colored markers

◎ Timer

INSTRUCTIONS

Have a breath and open your heart to serve as a channel for love. Set the timer for twenty minutes and use the index cards and markers provided to create loving, inspirational messages to be left for strangers. Write whatever message comes to your heart, for example, "You are beautiful," "I hope you know how loved you are," or "You can do it!" You may wish to decorate your notes with drawings or doodles as well. Later, as mother and daughter together, leave these inspirational notes in random places, such as a grocery store shelf, inside the pages of a library book, the mirror in a public bathroom, a bus stop bench, or on a car's windshield. It feels good to practice kindness!

Allow time for the circle to share the notes they created and where they think they might leave them to be found.

Temporary Butterfly Tattoos

Have you ever heard of The Butterfly Effect? In a field of mathematics called Chaos Theory, The Butterfly Effect is a metaphorical example of the details of a hurricane being influenced by minor perturbations, such as the flapping of the wings of a distant butterfly several weeks earlier. The scientific theory that a single occurrence, no matter how small, can change the course of the universe forever is an inspiring idea to consider as we contemplate this month's mantra, "I Am Changing the World."

As heroines, we know that one act of love, no matter how quiet, can change a person's day—even his or her whole life! To remind ourselves of this truth, members of the circle will apply temporary butterfly tattoos to the top of their hands, or anywhere else on their body they chose. Each time you see your butterfly, let it be a reminder that you, beloved sister, are changing the world.

SUPPLIES

◎ Butterfly temporary tattoos. One for each circle member.

◎ Small bowls of water (or other water source.)

◎ Sponges (or absorbent paper towels.)

Serve Together

As a circle, chose a service project to complete together this month. Volunteering together helps forge stronger ties among circle members, empowers mothers and daughters, and helps communities—all at the same time! It's a win-win-win! Your circle may wish to spend an afternoon volunteering at the local food pantry or animal shelter, picking up litter off the street, or collecting items to donate to the local homeless shelter. The options are limitless!

Medicine Meditation

Set your things to the side, find a comfortable, fully-supported resting position, perhaps take your mother's hand if that would feel good to you, and begin to follow your breath. In your mind's eye, see Mother Teresa. She is a tiny woman, not quite five feet tall. A simple, white sari with blue stripes frames her face and shrouds her body. Her dark eyes command attention, radiating energy of strength and intelligence. A warm smile spreads across her beautifully wrinkled face as she slowly walks toward you, extending her arms. She takes your hands firmly in hers and looks deep into your eyes. What words or phrases come to your mind or fill your heart as you look into the eyes of this wise woman? What question do you most want to ask her? Go ahead. Ask her and listen to her reply. Send your love and gratitude back to Mother Teresa, perhaps offering her a hug if that would feel good to you, and when you are ready, open your eyes.

Quote Study

"If we have no peace, it is because we have forgotten that we belong to each other."

"Spread love everywhere you go. Let no one ever come to you without leaving happier."

"Besides the poverty, material poverty . . . that makes the people die of hunger, die of cold, die in the streets—there is that great poverty of being unwanted, unloved, uncared for, having no one to call your own, having no one to smile . . . that poverty comes right there, in our own home, we even neglect to love. This is the great poverty and I think unless and until we begin to love at home . . . we cannot hope for peace."

"Love begins at home, and it is not how much we do . . . but how much love we put in the action that we do."

"Intense love does not measure, it just gives."

"We ourselves feel that what we are doing is just a drop in the ocean, but if that drop was not in the ocean, I think the ocean would be less because of that missing drop."

"I never look at the masses as my responsibility. I look at the individual. I can only love one person at a time—just one, one, one . . . "

Recommended Resources

Books for Mothers and Daughters, Ages 7+

Mother Teresa, by Demi

Who Was Mother Teresa? By Gigliotti, J.

Books for Mothers and Daughters, Ages 12+

Mother Teresa: A Life Inspired, by North, W.

Mother Teresa: An Authorized Biography, by Sprink, K.

Film for Mothers and Daughters, Ages 7+

Mother Teresa: An Animated Classic (2013)

Film for Mothers and Daughters, Ages 12+

Mother Teresa (2007)

Music

"Mother Teresa's Song" by Tompkins, L.

Web

www.notablebiographies.com/Mo-Ni/Mother-Teresa.html

Additional Recommended Resources for Mothers

The World Needs Your Kid: Raising Children Who Care and Contribute, by Kielburger, C.

A New Earth: Awakening to Your Life's Purpose, by Tolle, E.

PARTING WORDS

Dear Mothers,

It is my deepest hope that you have found inspiration and support in the pages of this book. Empowerment is a gift that we as mothers **can** give our daughters, and you, beloved woman, **can** do this! You already have within you all the tools and skills needed to create your own Heroines Club circle and lead your daughter, yourself, and your community of women, on a journey to even fuller empowerment. Sharing the Heroines Club with your daughter will place an anchor so deep in her heart, that someday if she drifts . . . she can only drift so far. And by blessing your daughter in this way, you will further heal yourself.

Our daughters need us and we are the ones we have been waiting for.

We are in this together.

Love,
Melia

We don't need someone to show us the ropes. We are the ones we've been waiting for. Deep inside us we know the feelings we need to guide us. Our task is to learn to trust our inner knowing.

Sonia Johnson

ABOUT THE AUTHOR

MELIA KEETON-DIGBY M.Ed, author of *The Heroines Club: A Mother-Daughter Empowerment Circle,* is a mother of three, speech-language pathologist, transformational life coach, author, blogger, and sacred circle facilitator who brings the nourishing medicine of the Great Mother into all she does.

She is the founder of The Mother-Daughter Nest, a sacred women's gathering space nestled in a cozy sanctuary among the trees on her family's land just outside the magical town of Athens, Georgia, US. The Mother-Daughter Nest lovingly offers sacred women's circles, mother-daughter circles, rites of passage ceremonies, workshops, and a variety of coaching services to women, mothers, and mothers and daughters together. It is the birthplace of the original Heroines Club Empowerment Circle.

Melia is passionately invested in supporting mothers to raise confident, connected daughters. On a daily basis, she demonstrates an acute ability to guide and support parents and their children to reach their highest potential, cultivated through more than a decade of experience working with children of all ages in the public school system as well as a complete devotion to the ancient practice of women circling together. She brings a holistic perspective to her work and writes extensively about mothering, daughtering, and the beautiful, often complex, mother-daughter relationship. Her work has been featured in a variety of online and print publications.

For further resources, print-ready resources and support, please join her at:

www.theheroinesclub.com

www.themotherdaughternest.com

Facebook/The Heroines Club

Facebook/The Mother-Daughter Nest

For individual mentoring, speaking engagements, or guest facilitation, please contact her by email at:

melia@theheroinesclub.com

ABOUT THE ARTIST

ARNA BAARTZ is an artist, educator and poet who created the artwork featured on the cover of *The Heroines Club*. She has been finger-painting from the beginning when her father encouraged her by taping paper to the walls of their home and letting her loose with paint. As a result, she is an expressive artist with a belief in non-judgement, often purposely leaving her 'mistakes' in an attempt to allow the unfolding to participate in a finished piece.

Most of Arna's work is an extension of her philosophical nature, bringing her gifts of personal insight and joy. She works in her bush studio everyday, surrounded by weird Australian wildlife, inspired by the connection between things and the glow of the rainforest.

The perfume of the valley permeates Arna's work and keeps her alive, as does her lovely, supportive husband and eight wonderful children.

www.arnabaartz.com   www.artofkundalini.com

Womancraft
PUBLISHING

Life-changing, paradigm-shifting books
by women, for women

Visit us at www.womancraftpublishing.com
where you can sign up to the mailing list and receive samples of
our forthcoming titles before anyone else.

(f) Womancraft Publishing   (y) WomancraftBooks

(o) Womancraft Publishing

If you have enjoyed this book, please leave a review
on Amazon or Goodreads.

Also from WOMANCRAFT PUBLISHING

The Heart of the Labyrinth,
by Nicole Schwab (November 2014)

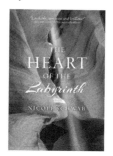

Reminiscent of Paulo Coelho's masterpiece *The Alchemist* and Lynn V. Andrew's acclaimed *Medicine Woman* series, *The Heart of the Labyrinth* is a beautifully evocative spiritual parable, filled with exotic landscapes and transformational soul lessons.

Once in a while, a book comes along that kindles the fire of our inner wisdom so profoundly, the words seem to leap off the page and go straight into our heart. If you read only one book this year, this is it.

Dean Ornish, M.D., President, Preventive Medicine Research Institute, Clinical Professor of Medicine, University of California, Author of *The Spectrum*

Moods of Motherhood: the inner journey of mothering,
by Lucy H. Pearce (November 2014)

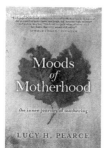

Moods of Motherhood charts the inner journey of motherhood, giving voice to the often nebulous, unspoken tumble of emotions that motherhood evokes: tenderness, frustration, joy, grief, anger, depression and love.

Lucy's frank and forthright style paired with beautiful, haunting language and her talent for storytelling will have any parent nodding, crying and laughing along – appreciating the good and the bad, the hard and the soft, the light and the dark. A must-read for any new parent.

Zoe Foster, JUNO magazine

Moon Time: harness the ever-changing energy of your menstrual cycle,
by Lucy H. Pearce (June 2015)

Hailed as 'life-changing' by women around the world, *Moon Time* shares a fully embodied understanding of the menstrual cycle. Full of practical insight, empowering resources, creative activities and passion, this book will put women back in touch with their body's wisdom. Amazon #1 bestseller in Menstruation.

Lucy, your book is monumental. The wisdom in Moon Time sets a new course where we glimpse a future culture reshaped by honoring our womanhood journeys one woman at a time.

ALisa Starkweather, author and founder of Red Tent Temple Movement

Reaching for the Moon: a girl's guide to her cycles,
by Lucy H. Pearce (October 2015)

The girls' version of Lucy H. Pearce's Amazon bestselling book *Moon Time*. For girls aged 9-14, as they anticipate and experience their body's changes. *Reaching for the Moon* is a nurturing celebration of a girl's transformation to womanhood.

A message of wonder, empowerment, magic and beauty in the shared secrets of our femininity . . . written to encourage girls to embrace their transition to womanhood in a knowledgeable, supported, loving way.

THELOVINGPARENT.COM

***The Other Side of the River: Stories of Women, Water and the World*,**
by Eila Kundrie Carrico (January 2016)

A deep searching into the ways we become dammed and how we recover fluidity. It is a journey through memory and time, personal and shared landscapes to discover the source, the flow and the deltas of women and water.

Part memoir, part manifesto, part travelogue and part love letter to myth and ecology, *The Other Side of the River* is an intricately woven tale of finding your flow . . . and your roots.

An instant classic for the new paradigm.
Lucia Chivola Birnbaum, award-winning author and Professor Emeritus

***Burning Woman*,**
by Lucy H. Pearce (May 2016)

The long-awaited new title from Amazon bestselling author Lucy H. Pearce. *Burning Woman* is a breath-taking and controversial woman's journey through history— personal and cultural—on a quest to find and free her own power.

This incendiary text was written for women who burn with passion, have been burned with shame, and who at another time, in another place, would have been burned at the stake. With contributions from leading burning women of our era: Isabel Abbott, ALisa Starkweather, Shiloh Sophia McCloud, Molly Remer, Julie Daley, Bethany Webster . . .

***Liberating Motherhood: Birthing the Purplestockings Movement*,**
by Vanessa Oleronshaw (September 2016)

***Birthing Ourselves into Being*,**
by Baraka Elihu and Autumn Weaver (October 2016)

Printed in Great Britain
by Amazon